Peripheral Light

Selected and New Poems

Also by John Kinsella

Poems
  The Hierarchy of Sheep
  Zone
  Visitants
  The Benefaction
  The Hunt
  Poems 1980–1994
  Graphology
  Lightning Tree
  The Undertow
  The Radnoti Poems
  The Silo: A Pastoral Symphony
  Erratum/Frame(d)
  Syzygy
  Full Fathom Five
  Eschatologies
  Night Parrots

Fiction
  Grappling Eros
  Genre

Drama
  Divinations: Four Plays

Autobiography
  Auto

Peripheral Light

Selected and New Poems

JOHN KINSELLA

Selected and with an Introduction by
Harold Bloom

W. W. NORTON & COMPANY • NEW YORK LONDON

For information about permission to reproduce selections from this book, write to
Permissions, W. W. Norton & Company, Inc., 500 Fifth Avenue, New York, NY 10110

Manufacturing by Quebecor Fairfield
Book design by Carole Goodman
Production manager: Julia Druskin

Library of Congress Cataloging-in-Publication Data

Kinsella, John, 1963–
Peripheral light : selected and new poems / John Kinsella ;
introduced by Harold Bloom.— 1st ed.
p. cm.
Includes bibliographical references and index.
ISBN 0-393-05821-2 (hardcover)
I. Title.
PR9619.3.K55P47 2004
821'.914—dc22

2003016738

W. W. Norton & Company, Inc.
500 Fifth Avenue, New York, N.Y. 10110
www.wwnorton.com

W. W. Norton & Company Ltd.
Castle House, 75/76 Wells Street, London W1T 3QT

1 2 3 4 5 6 7 8 9 0

for Harold and Tracy, with thanks

Contents

Introduction . . . . *xiii*

LINKS 3

FINCHES 5

CRANE AND HAWK 7

BLACK SUNS 8

INLAND 9

OLD HANDS/NEW TRICKS 11

TWO DAYS BEFORE HARVEST 12

THE MYTH OF THE GRAVE 13

PILLARS OF SALT 15

PIPELINE 17

THE ORCHARDIST 18

THE BOTTLEBRUSH FLOWERS 19

PLUMBURST 20

ECLOGUE ON A WELL 21

WHEATBELT GOTHIC OR DISCOVERING A WYETH 22

SKIPPY ROCK, AUGUSTA: WARNING, THE UNDERTOW 23

CHILLI CATHARSIS 26

ON ENTERING YOUR THIRTY-FIRST YEAR 27

WARHOL AT WHEATLANDS 30

THE ASCENSION OF SHEEP 32

SCULPTING A POEM FROM THE LANDSCAPE'S PAINTING 33

ROCK PICKING: BUILDING CAIRNS 36

POEM FOR THOSE AT WHEATLANDS 38

The Silo 39

Why They Stripped the Last Trees 41

Fog 42

Goading Storms Out of a Darkening Field 44

Parrot Deaths: Rites of Passage 45

Skeleton weed/generative grammar 46

Bluff Knoll Sublimity 48

Of Writing at Wheatlands 50

Anathalamion 54

Lightning Tree 57

Approaching the Anniversary of my
Last Meeting with my Son 58

Grave 60

Tenebrae 61

Solitary Activities 62

Wild Radishes 63

Drowning in Wheat 64

The Hunt 66

An Aerial View of Wheatlands in Mid-Autumn 69

The Machine of the Twentieth Century 71

Skylab and The Theory of Forms 73

The Bermuda Triangle 75

The Road to Brookton — on the nature of memory . . . 76

After Sir Lawrence Alma-Tadema's 79

Hockney's *Doll Boy* 80

Shoes once shod in a blacksmith's shop 82

Il faut cultiver notre jardin 83

Hectic Red 85

drought 87

Funeral Oration 88

Hölderlin was not Mad 89

Sanctus, Sanctum: a love poem 96

Sine qua non 99

The Branches 100

Field Notes from Mount Bakewell 101

The Predominance of Red 109

A Cardinal Influences Peripheral Sight 111

Lyrical Unification in Gambier 112

Diagnostics 114

Cultures 115

The Chambers 116

House Eclogue 120

Poltergeist House Eclogue 123

The Gift 125

First Essay on Linguistic Disobedience 126

Second Essay on Linguistic Disobedience 129

Third Essay on Linguistic Disobedience 132

Fourth Essay on Linguistic Disobedience 134

Fifth Essay on Linguistic Disobedience 136

Sixth Essay on Linguistic Disobedience 138

Seventh Essay on Linguistic Disobedience 141

The Shed 143

Through Vertical Blinds 146

The Trial 148

The Semiotics of a Truck Overturned in Fog 150

On the Rejection of the Term "Property"
for This Place 151

The Crest 154

Hay Bale Collected Off Road 155

Lighting the Bushman Fire Before the Others Rise . 157

Boustrophedon 159

The Burning of the Hay Stacks 161

Salt Lesson 163

Chainsaw 164

Against Depression 166

The Early Onset of Darkness 167

Land Leased Back to Themselves 168

Miracle at New Norcia 171

Imitations of Sign and Subjectivity in York 173

The View 177

Location Triggers 178

Across the Gravel Wastes 180

Mulga Parrots 181

Flight 182

The Killing Tree 184

Removing the Fox Baits 186

Cold 187

Aftershocks 188

Liminal Devotional 189

Index of Titles and First Lines 191

Acknowledgments for Previously Uncollected Poems

The Age

Agni

Angelaki

Antipodes

The Australian

Australian Book Review

Boston Review

Copper Tales

Georgia Review

The Guardian

Jacket

The Kenyon Review

Kunapipi

Moving Worlds: A Journal of Transcultural Writings

The Literary Review

Near East Review

New England Review

North American Review

Poetry

Poetry London

Poetry New Zealand

Poetry Review

The Republic of Letters

Seneca Review

Southerly

Verse

Webdelsol

The Yale Review

Introduction

JOHN KINSELLA IS AN ORPHIC FOUNTAIN, a prodigy of the imagination. Despite his deep rootedness in Australian literary culture, he frequently makes me think of John Ashbery: improbable fecundity, eclecticism, and a stand that fuses populism and elitism in poetic audience.

I start with early Kinsella, the lyric "Crane and Hawk":

> The crane, eyes fixed, moves steadily,
> its expression one of quiet desperation;
> awkwardly graceful, it lifts
> with an arc of its wings.
>
> Turning and cutting the same path over,
> the crane relies on what *we* know as *patience*,
> while the hawk effortlessly shadows—
> death's mimic playing with time.
>
> Between the two, a world rife
> with speculation turns uneasily
> on its tightening axis; within,
> there is something too perfect.
>
> The shudder of the crane stretching,
> (the rhetoric of expectation?),
> could be an updraft seized mid-flight
> and fallen by the way . . .
>
> What end when a bird of prey
> moves so slowly? When a crane would seek
> no more than a circuitous life anyway,
> and the day warms to indifference.

These are the contraries in Kinsella's rhetoric: his heart is with the crane's "rhetoric of expectation," while his mind chooses the hawk's shadowing rhetoric that defeats expectation with mortality. A country man, Kinsella is most at ease with natural emblems: they mediate mortality for him, as here, in "The Myth of the Grave":

> A pair of painted quails
> scurries across the quills of stubble
> a flurry of rapid
> eye movement
>
> they shadow my walk
> ostentatiously
> lifting and dropping
> into invisible alleyways
>
> reaching the grave
> I turn to catch them
> curving back, stopped
> by the windrows
>
> the grave is a magnet
> that switches polarity
> when you reach it.

The shadowing is of the essence. What surprises me is the dark wit of the poem's final section:

> A fresh grave that holds three
> generations is something you question
> on a first encounter. How in life
> would they have felt about sharing
> a single room in a shoebox flat?
> Maybe, at an instant, only one soul

is resident, the others entering the bodies
of quails, exploring the wastes of stubble.

The "pair of painted quails" are waiting their turn in the "shoe-box flat." Ashes do not rest easily in Kinsella, for whom the dead are not dead, but alive. There aren't any natural vistas among Kinsella's many landscapes; they are all haunted, part of the under-tow, as at "Skippy Rock, Augusta": "dusk-spray, undertow/ of night." A sleepless soul, akin to Wordsworth's Thomas Chatterton in "Resolution and Independence," Kinsella is addicted to red chili, rather in the way that D. H. Lawrence sought out medlars and sorb-apples. The Lawrence of *Birds, Beasts, and Flowers* is never far from Kinsella: both poets long for Persephone. Only John Kinsella could transcendentalize a chili pepper.

For some years, I have argued against Deconstruction by asking the question: how does meaning ever get started, rather than just repeated? I have found my answer in Shakespearean excess: Falstaff, Hamlet, Iago, Lear, Cleopatra. The implicit metaphysic of Kinsella's poetry *is* excess, congruent with a personal energy so excessive that he cannot rest. That is the humor of his "On Entering Your Thirty-First Year," and underlies his curious attachments to Dennis Hopper and to Warhol, who do not move me. Kinsella's mordant comedy however holds on in me, as in that weird poem, "The Ascension of Sheep":

> The sun has dragged
> the fog away
> and now the sheep
> in sodden clothes may
>
> fleece the farmer—
> who warm by the fire
> tallies heads and prices
> and thinks about slaughter—

each soul taken upwards
from its fertile
body—columns of mist
like pillars of a temple.

Come midday they'll
have dried right through
and follow the trail
down to the dam

where the water
refills the empty chamber
where the soul
could never feel secure.

This uncanny piece is unlike anything else I know, even by Kinsella, or perhaps I should call it an unique ascension. Ascension, secularized, is one of Kinsella's creative obsessions. Australia is (and will be) permanently undiscovered country for me, but as Kinsella's constant reader I begin to sense that the abyss of the outback is a condition of his poetry, a frame that enables it to continue. His cairns are "pyramids of the outback," the setting for a pastoral poetry that triumphs in "The Silo":

Visitors, as if they knew, never remarked
on the old silo with its rammed earth walls
and high thatched roof, incongruous amongst
the new machinery and silver field bins.
Nor the workers brought in at harvest time,
trucks rolling past the ghostly whimperings,
snarls and sharp howls cutting the thick silo's
baffling. Nor when a bumper harvest filled
every bin and the farmer was hungry
for space—no one ever mentioned bringing

the old silo back into service. This
had been the way for as far back as could
be remembered. Thin sprays of baby's breath
grew around its foundations, while wedding
bouquet sprouted bizarrely from the grey
mat of thatching. The sun had bleached the walls
bone-white while the path to the heavily
bolted door was of red earth, a long thin
stream of unhealthy blood. Before those storms
which brew thickly on summer evenings
red-tailed black cockatoos settled in waves,
sparking the straw like a volcano, dark
fire erupting from the heart of the white
silo, trembling with energy deeper
than any anchorage earth could offer.
And lightning dragging a moon's bleak halo
to dampen the eruption, with thunder
echoing out over the bare paddocks
towards the farmhouse where an old farmer
consoled his bitter wife on the fly-proof
verandah, cursing the cockatoos, hands
describing a prison from which neither
could hope for parole, petition, release.

This is the hawk's vision, not the crane's and the old silo is a ver-
itable tower of mortality, a temple of the Reality Principle. What
makes the poem Kinsellan are those vitalizing cockatoos, trembling
with more than natural energy. I think again of Lawrence, but now
in an unlikely alliance with Robert Frost. "The Silo," a permanent
poem, makes space for itself by putting a fine pressure upon mod-
ern pastoral, from Thomas Hardy onwards.

Kinsella, in his country youth, seems to have shot so many
predatory parrots that their souls will haunt his way into Purgatory.
The best of these hauntings is "Parrot Deaths: Rites of Passage":

Blue clouds scuttle the eucalypt sun
as it fizzes and winces with impending
rain, sultry weather dampening
the orange hearts of king parrots.

The scimitar roads cull the golden grain
from dump trucks and belly spillers, tarps
tethered loosely, illegal loads shifting
over axles tense with excess tonnage.

Rosellas gather about the grain offerings
and the torn bodies of the fallen. Wood smoke
hustles a magpie lark out of an uncharacteristic
torpor. A crow hangs low and watches intently.

Observing the rites of passage a regent
parrot plunges into the dead eyes of a semi,
eyes of silver nitrate, tarnished and stained
shadow black. The orange, golden and emerald

hearts of parrots litter the roads. I drive
slowly and whisper prayers of deflection.

Most poems by Kinsella are secular "prayers of deflection,"
since he knows the truth of Emerson's "Self-Reliance":

> As men's prayers are a disease of the will, so are their
> creeds a
> disease of the intellect.

One sees why Kinsella testifies that Frost's "Birches" have held
him since first reading, offering a vision of "both going and com-
ing back." Everything in Kinsella's nature is "Ceremony.

Massacre. Survey." That is a strong burden for pastoral, but without it Kinsella's poetry would not take on its real importance. He is a celebrant of the rueful Sublime, exemplifying both Ruskin's strictures against the Pathetic Fallacy and Ruskin's contradictory realization that a poet is a person "to whom things speak." That is the rugged achievement of "Bluff Knoll Sublimity" and "Of Writing at Wheatlands," two of Kinsella's finest.

Kinsella, whether he sojourns in Cambridgeshire or in Ohio, always finds himself going home to the wheatlands and pastures of his childhood, returns remarkably free both from nostalgia and from guilt. Here is the first verse stanza of "Anathalamion," one of Kinsella's central visions:

My parents dead & the family property
broken up, I live on *their* place—in the old shearing
quarters—& keep an eye on things. Talking
business with the old man is impossible though the old lady
comes to the quarters once a week & we sit with a cuppa
  & study
the week's takings—sorting out the bills & tallying
the red & black figures. She's always been good
with numbers. But it's like she's given up caring
about things really—just working the sums to trade
away the bad memories. The old man sits in a hide
down by the creek some days—watching the blue heron
high in the redgum tree that was blasted
by lightning years back. When I go to the hotel
they ask me what the old couple do these days but I just
  get plastered
& stare into my beer—snubbing even the mayor—'to Hell
with the lot of you!' I'll yell, just waiting for a quarrel.
On a dark day, when the season was closing in,
they were seen leaving the town, like the blue heron.

There aren't any other anathalamia, not that I know of, anyway. What is being cursed here, or assigned to damnation? Certainly not the old people, or the obsession with the blue heron:

> After their son's death the blue heron became the old man's obsession and his wife told me he only ever spoke to her when talking of them. The blue heron, their nest raided by crows, have left the redgum this year. I like to think they're nesting nearby—maybe further upcreek where the redgums are still thick. Their son had once claimed that he'd been told by a hay stooker that if you died near a heron your soul joined with its soul. He'd told that to his parents and they'd laughed. He marvelled that it was called a blue heron when it was more of a grey colour. On a dark day, when the season was closing in, they were seen leaving the town, like the blue heron.

In this vibrant alternation of verse and prose stanzas, the second verse-section raises us to the level of painfulness that might justify an anathema:

> As children we'd burrow into the hay
> or move bales like building blocks, trapping
> carpet snakes. Together saw Tad Hunter clutching
> at the mangled stump of his arm, the auger crazy
> with his blood. Once we nearly drowned in a silo of barley,
> sinking further with every move, pulled out crying
> by his old man who said we'd learnt our lesson & didn't need
> punishing any further. Who said the same, when—riding
> his motorbike—we hit the cattle grid & skewed
> into the creek. And when we fed a pet sheep his premium seed
> wheat & watched it die from pickle poisoning. Neighbours
> called us feral kids—'little bastards, getting their claws
> into everythin', like locusts in the crop, nothin' can stop

'em.' It's true, we ran amok, but we did our chores
& didn't mean any harm—a chip
off the ol' block his dad would say to the town cop.
On a dark day, when the season was closing in,
they were seen leaving the town, married again.

Of the four refrains, only this third, and the fifth substitute
"married again" for "like the blue heron." The remarriage or rec-
onciliation prompts anathalamion, since it is the bereftness of the
old couple that contrasts throughout with the shamanistic emblem
of survival, fusion with the soul of the blue heron:

In some ways it was like a world under glass—porous
glass that let in the creek and the birds and the weather
and the children who'd creep up to the house as a dare,
the old people having *that* reputation for strangeness,
but kept the pain in, petrified in the moment. The boy's
death had cut it off from the outside world and it existed
in a twilight which not even the most determined sea-
sons could breach. I never said much about him. I read
a lot and kept to myself. But even the brightest
books seemed dull. The shadows of the blue heron
indelible on their pages. On a dark day, when the sea-
son was closing in, they were seen leaving the town,
like the blue heron.

The shadows of the blue heron return us to hawk-shadow in
Kinsella. Yeats played with the same shamanism, yet Kinsella wins
his gamble in this verse/prose poem, dangerous as it is to go too
near to Yeats. So strong is the poem's conclusion that I am moved
to call this the true voice of John Kinsella:

It was one of those days when the black
cockatoos were low-loping in a storm-stained sky
& the creek ran river-thick, scouring the red clay

banks & swamping the nests of water rats, & the track
up to the top gate was up to the axles with mud & a long trek
around the flooded paddocks was necessary, stray
sheep stuck firm, the silos damp & full of sprouted wheat,
that they both emerged in black raincoats & doggedly
made their way to town on foot. As word had spread, the
  main street
was lined with adults & children who thought they were in
  for a treat.
But the old couple didn't lift their heads, & neither led
the other as they marched like mourners or a parody of
  the dead,
marching a slow funereal slog towards the empty church.
A few moments later the priest appeared
& followed them into the silence beyond the arch.
On a dark day when the season was closing in,
they were seen leaving the town, married again.

It is as grim a remarriage as might be imagined, almost as though the living dead joined again. What begins to clarify is that Kinsella's great originality is not in matters of form, stance, and style (though he has strengths in all those) but in sensibility and temperament. He perceives and senses almost occultly: if there still be, this late, a "pure" poet, it would be him, free of ideologies and of any histories that are not personal. Perhaps there cannot be a pure poet, but I would offer his "Lightning Tree" as a pure poem:

It's stark white in this hard
winter light. At its base
brackish water spreads like exposed film
out through marshgrass & paperbarks—
a snapped bone, it punctures the skin.
On its splintered crown
the Great Egret stretches, its knifed beak

piercing the cold blue sky—
an inverted lightning strike
fielding its wings—
a crucifix—hesitating,
as if held by a magnet,
then dropping into flight,
dragging lightning rod legs.

That is sensation and perception in Walter Pater's Epicurean
mode. The metaphysical materialism nevertheless is qualified by
"splintered crown" and "crucify," images ultimately suggesting that
"Lightning Tree" could be an emblem of resurrection. Whatever
his stoic skepticism, Kinsella knows himself to live willingly on
faultlines. A poet of deep subjectivity, like Stevens and Ashbery,
Kinsella understands that "confessional" poetry leaves both poet
and reader more opaque than before, whereas total revelation, of
self and of other, emerges from difficult art, as here in "Tenebrae":

You are on the verge
of a resurrection,
standing on a fragile shoreline,
erosion undermining
the limestone cliff face,
expecting to plunge suddenly
into the churning ocean.
You'd rebuild memories,
though this coastline
is always changing—a childhood
hiding place eroded,
an overhang collapsed
like the tide. Those
limestone columns
reaching towards a god
that would take your past

as if it were an offering.
But though the lights
one by one extinguish
as you explore deeper,
that final light—the sun—
grows stronger,
despite the coming winter,
the darkening seas.

This tribute to his wife's poetry is also Kinsella's *ars poetica*. The mode is Wordsworthian, searching childhood for the hiding place of one's power; the form has an aura of Yeats about it. Yet the displacement of Catholic ritual counts for more. We hear a praise-song, as towards the close of Holy Week. The ceremonial candles of the Tenebrae go out one by one, and the final light, the sun of poetry and of resurrection, poetic *or* Christian, grows stronger. I associate this triumphal meditation with two much darker poems, "Approaching the Anniversary of my Last Meeting with my Son," and "Grave," which have something of the same splendor of a total clarity.

Multiplying instances of Kinsella's epiphanies will not lead me further into what makes his best work so distinctive. I halt therefore before a brief lyric that has placed me under a spell since first I read it, "Wild Radishes":

Across the dark fields the family is spread
While overhead the sky is haunted,
In the dull light they scour the crop
Never looking up as the day seems to stop.
Wild radishes missed will destroy the yield—
Bills to be paid, deals to be sealed.
But the plover's refusal to lift and drop,

And the absence of crow and parrot talk,
And the immense racket as stalk rubs on stalk,

Register somewhere deep in the soul.
And as the sun begins to uncoil—
The deep green of the wheat uneasy with light—
The golden flowers of wild radishes bite
Just before they are ripped from the soil.

This is the quintessence of John Kinsella, equally populist and elitist. I think of John Clare and of other "peasant-poets." If there is such a genre as peasant-poetry, of the most sophisticated kind, could it be more beautifully exemplified? The interplay of dulled light and muted sound intimates a more profound interchange, between familial past and an art ripped from both soil and soul.

I used to think of John Kinsella as being one of the poets who unfolded, like Hart Crane, rather than one of those who developed, like Wallace Stevens. This distinction I derive from the late Northrop Frye, who did not make a shibboleth of it. In the last five to seven years, Kinsella has developed extraordinarily. I juxtapose two poems, the beautiful Hardyesque "An Aerial View of Wheatlands in Mid-Autumn," with the more recent "A Cardinal Influences Peripheral Sight." Here is the last stanza of "An Aerial View . . ." set against a part of the Celanesque "Peripheral Sight":

Is not the harmony of this decade.
Instead look to the flux of soil and fire,
The low loping flight of the darkest bird,
The frantic dash of the land-bound plover,
The breaking of salt by errant samphire,
The flow of water after steady rain,
The everlasting in bright disorder,
The stealthy path of the predating plane
Cutting boundaries as you sow your grain.

✦

We see community
and politics in the starlings'
feeding frenzy, hearted
deep by cardinal

working outwards,
its influence equally
peripheral through
the gridwork,

a blurring that bleeds
cross-species.
The failure of this
transcendent interlude

to contain colour
or snow glare
within the black reflector,
bares molten feathers,
blood vessels woven together.

Is it the same poet? The harvester, Kinsella's firmest identity, yields
to the alienated Celan-like spectator, for whom every natural context
comes apart, even as no social context ever can come together again.
Kinsella is in movement towards becoming a very different poet, able
to balance personal loss with at least the possibility of a more univer-
sal art, founded upon rejection of an earlier imaginative idealism:

Poetry is a crematorium.
Love doesn't need it.

As a final text here, indicating the ongoing Kinsella, I take the
very ambitious sixteen-part sequence "Field Notes from Mount

Bakewell," which is a kind of holy mountain for Kinsella. Upon his high places, Kinsella finds, not apotheosis, but ecological ruin:

> . . . aerial mimics,
> clarifiers of vegetable harmonics,
> telecommunication dishes
> microwaving panoramically,
> ingesting and feeding
> the collective soul.

Against this, there are predatory intimations that are ancient: locusts, who have tracked Kinsella throughout his work. But they arrive now into a world of insurance companies and medical certificates:

> Genetically engineered crops
> are sweeping the district.
> This corn grows steadily, daily.
> The locusts have come. Let
> them eat corn, he says, let them strip
> the green before the seeds
> have even come. They have
> no choice, and I have no choice.
> The insurance company
> twists and turns, lies, hedges
> its bets. Medical certificates
> shoot the breeze. The locusts
> tune in and out, changing frequencies.
> No, they don't tell
> the same story.

The final vision of Mount Bakewell marks the end of Kinsella's Australian pastoral:

Place of weeping, sleeping woman,
eloping against tradition
and cursed from bloodshed,
across the town,
across the region,
not hearing the warning,
the passion, the bleeding:
the mountains
breaking up and meeting,
reconciled as erosion
defeats them.

The poignance of this marks the end of one mode of poetry, pastoral in the last ditch, and the coming-on of something different and darker. At this midpoint of a remarkable career, Kinsella needs to be read in something of his prodigal profusion, the generous scattering of his gifts. We are poised before the onset of what I prophesy will be a major art:

a call cuts a blank space,
a place where the blackest branches
drag sight, where song birds
were brought before dark,
when the owl was silent.

HAROLD BLOOM

Peripheral Light

Links

'Every separation is a link . . .'
—Simone Weil

i
There are days when the world
buckles under the sun, trees blacken
to thin wisps, spinifex fires,
and white cockatoos, strangled
in telegraph wire, hang
dry and upside down.

ii
I think only of thirst.
The drifting sand does not
lend itself to description,
the sketchy border trees
offer little protection
from the sun as we negotiate
the edge and fine line
between sand and vegetation.

iii
I have always lived by the sea,
or travelling underground, have always
been concerned with water—the flooding
of mines, rain in dark forests,
the level of the tide.

iv

To see a waterbird, maybe a crane,
fly deep into desert, comes as no
surprise—we note its arrival and follow
its disappearance, discuss it over a beer,
and think nothing more of it.

v

And nights, contracting into cool winds,
when the sand becomes an astrolabe to the stars,
where in the reflection of the crystal spheres
we wander without direction, searching out
water flowers . . .

Finches

Salt Paddocks
Down below the dam
there is nothing but salt,
a slow encroachment.

Fighting back, my cousins
have surrounded it
with a ring of trees.

At its centre
lives a colony of finches,
buried in tamarisks.

Finch Colony
The leaves, like wire, are so tangled
we dare not venture too far into their heart
where flashes of song and dull colour
betray a whole family of finches.

We hold our breath
and become statues.

Is this fear of disturbing their peace
or of a delicate raid from unknown spaces?

Finch Flight
To join the finch
in his tenuous kingdom
amongst tamarisks,
the hot snow of salt

You must gather
trajectory and direction,
sharp summer flights

Exile yourself
from the wind's hand.

Finch Death
The dead finch lies on salt,
tight-winged and stretched.

The others shimmer
loosely in heat

the salt's white mystery
coveting tin cans, skull of sheep.

Slowly, death rides this hot glacier
further and further away.

Crane and Hawk

The crane, eyes fixed, moves steadily,
its expression one of quiet desperation;
awkwardly graceful, it lifts
with an arc of its wings.

Turning and cutting the same path over,
the crane relies on what *we* know as *patience*,
while the hawk effortlessly shadows—
death's mimic playing with time.

Between the two, a world rife
with speculation turns uneasily
on its tightening axis; within,
there is something too perfect.

The shudder of the crane stretching,
(the rhetoric of expectation?),
could be an updraft seized mid-flight
and fallen by the way . . .

What end when a bird of prey
moves so slowly? When a crane would seek
no more than a circuitous life anyway,
and the day warms to indifference.

Black Suns

The orchard, canker-bound and fading—Australian
Gothic. A bladeless windmill remonstrates

with a warm wind as it singes
oranges scattered in bitter wreaths

of deadwood, scale, and vitrified leaves.
A black-winged kite wrestles with temptation

and logic, water rats scaling the ruins
of barbed wire fences. The season equivocates.

I remove my shoes, the water stretches
bulrushes like new strings on an old guitar.

I position the wreck of my body and wait.
There is arrogance in this—expecting

him to appear, to consider his withering fruit,
divine my return, while refusing to cross

and help drag black suns from their sick zodiacs
with the hook of his walking-stick.

Inland

Inland: storm tides,
ghosts of a sheep weather
alert, the roads uncertain

families cutting the outback
gravel on Sunday mornings,
the old man plying the same track
to and from the session
those afternoons, evenings
(McHenry skidded into a thickset
mallee after a few too many
and was forced to sell up)

On the cusp of summer
an uncertain breeze
rises in grey wisps
over the stubble—
the days are ashen,
moods susceptible,
though it does not take
long to get back
into the swing of things

We take the only highroad
for miles as the centre
of the primum mobile—it's
the eye of the needle
through which our lives'
itineraries must be drawn,
a kind of stone theodolite
measuring our depths beyond

the straight and narrow,
it's a place of borrowed dreams
where the marks of the spirit
have been erased by dust—
the restless topsoil

Old Hands/New Tricks

A ring-necked parrot drops into flight,
fence-posts collapse and ossify,
the wattle bird trims the lamp of wattle bloom

Despite storm weather the soaks diminish,
though by way of contrast the green tinge
of a late rain pokes its head over stubble—
the new growth that will yield no seed

About the homestead unripe fruit is severed
from trees—parrots jostle, making
swings and see-saws of their bodies

The wells are covered with railway sleepers
over-run with wire-weed and Mediterranean
Bugloss—Salvation Jane—which crisps over
cracks, gives cool water a taste of irony

In the pepper trees magpies threaten to unpick
the world as they know it—their songs are not
characteristic—old hands have learnt new tricks

Two Days Before Harvest

An easterly stretches and compresses
deadwood fissures, strings of parakeets
arrange themselves into nets to drag
the breeze—their feathers firing,
the sun striking the afternoon pink.

In the soon-to-be-lopped heads of wheat
there burns the fidelity of summer—beyond,
on the white-bake of salt, lines of supply
are thinning and the dust of scuffed patches
drinks the blood of eucalypts. Topknot pigeons
encounter themselves, much to their surprise,
in foray from sheoak to powerline and back again.

The tines of a discarded scarifier have set
like the roots of trees ringbarked from memory—
you see, the tractor's welter, the jiggering
blades of the header, crows teasing
the gate-posts, unlock a continuity
that would persist, or threaten to . . .

The Myth of the Grave

i

A pair of painted quails
scurries across the quills of stubble
a flurry of rapid
eye movement

they shadow my walk
ostentatiously
lifting and dropping
into invisible alleyways

reaching the grave
I turn to catch them
curving back, stopped
by the windrows

the grave is a magnet
that switches polarity
when you reach it.

ii

The epitaph is measured
by the size of the plaque,
or is it the plaque that's
measured by the epitaph?

It seems to matter.
Death becomes a question
of economy—the lavish are big
on ceremony, slight on prayer.

iii

At a distance
sheep leave salt-licks
beside a dam and zig-zag
down towards the shade.

Grey gums bend with the tide
of the breeze, the midday sun
would carry their doubles
to the grave and fill the urns.

The ground dries and crumbles,
a lizard darts out of a crack
and races across the paddock.
Do ashes rest easily here?

iv

A fresh grave that holds three
generations is something you question
on a first encounter. How in life
would they have felt about sharing

a single room in a shoebox flat?
Maybe, at an instant, only one soul
is resident, the others entering the bodies
of quails, exploring the wastes of stubble.

Pillars of Salt

We always look back,
attracted by that feeling
of having been there before—the roads
sinking, the soil weeping (scab on scab
lifted), fences sunk to gullies
catching the garbage of paddocks,
strainers blocked by stubble
and machinery and the rungs
of collapsed rainwater tanks/and maybe
the chimney and fireplace
of a corroded farmhouse, once
the guts of the storm, now
a salty trinket.

The salt is a frozen waste
in a place too hot for its own good,
it is the burnt-out core of earth's eye,
the excess of white blood cells.
The ball-and-chain rides lushly
over its polishing surface, even dead wood
whittles itself out of the picture.

Salt crunches like sugar-glass, the sheets
lifting on the soles of shoes (thongs scatter
pieces beyond the hope of repair)—finches
and flies quibble on the thick fingers
of saltbushes, a dugite spits
blood into the brine.

An airforce trainer jet appears,
the mantis pilot—dark eyed and wire

jawed—sets sight on the white wastes
for a strafing run: diving, pulling out
abruptly, refusing to consummate.

                                 Salt
explodes silently, with the animation
of an inorganic life, a sheep's skull no more
than its signature, refugees already
climbing towards the sun
on pillars of salt.

Pipeline

The pipeline cleaves the catchment
with its good intention—on a watersling
outflowing the silver jacket, palmed
off by pumping station after pumping
station, though losing none of its spring,
darting forwards with a hop, skip, and a jump
riding sidecar to a national highway,
swinging from one climate to another
without a change of expression.
                              An egret flies
lower over a coastal reservoir, parrots
in unclaimed territory know the pipeline
to be a hot cable that will burn through claw,
a crow senses moisture at the final
pumping station.
                    In passing, it remains
indifferent to farm machinery, to the crisp
and wink of saltpans, to finches tossing
their hoods back and tittering
about its stiff shell.
                    In passing, it gloats inwardly
before leaving a dry wind that's been shooting
its skin to wrestle with scrub, before plunging
head first into red earth.

The Orchardist

Orange trees cling
to the tin walls
of his home. A red
checked shirt and grey
pair of trousers hang
over the one-eyed tractor.
His oranges are small suns
and he is an astronaut
floating slowly
through their spheres
of influence.

The Bottlebrush Flowers

A Council-approved replacement
for box trees along the verges
of suburban roads, it embarrasses
with its too sudden blush—stunning
at first, then a burning reminder
of something you'd rather forget.
And it unclothes so ungraciously—
its semi-clad, mangy, slovenly,
first-thing-in-the-morning appearance.
And while I've heard it called
a bristling firelick, a spiral
of Southern Lights, I've also seen
honey-eaters bob upside down
and unpick its light in seconds.

Plumburst

for Wendy

The neat greens of Monument Hill
roll into sea, over the rise the soft rain
of plumfall deceives us in its groundburst.

If lightning strikes from the ground up,
and Heaven is but an irritation that prompts
its angry spark, then plums are born
dishevelled on the ground and rise
towards perfection . . .

Out of the range of rising plums
we mark the territory of the garden,
testing caprock with Judas trees,
pacing out melon runs. Behind us a block
of flats hums into dusk and the sun
bursts a plum mid-flight.

Eclogue on a Well

She stirs the waters
breaking the stone rust surface;
if the branch she holds
were longer she might
bring proof to the claim
that more than one surface
lies beneath. Even so, I defer
to her belief that the One
is solid ground—the reflection
of a deep well in a dry field.

Wheatbelt Gothic or Discovering a Wyeth

Outflanked by the sheep run, wild oats
dry and riotous, barbed wire bleeding rust
over fence-posts, even quartz chunks
flaking with a lime canker, the theme
chooses itself: *ubi sunt* motif, but the verse
becomes as deceptive as an idle plough,
or a mat of hay spread over the ooze
of a dead sheep that is the floor
of the soak (blood-black beneath the skin,
bones honeycombed), crystallised with salt.

And yesteryear occluded by the viscous waters
of the stone-walled well which (on higher
ground) marks the dryness of the soak as either
delusion or lie. Only green shoots hidden
in the dead sheaths of reeds on the soak's rim
hint that water supports this travesty.

And the moon absorbs the sun, its fabric
subtlety—the undressing of a summer landscape
too blond for its own good, too much an extract:
the mid-West Gothic of a lone tree stump
that appears to beckon in its loneliness—open space
as collusive as a vaulted cathedral in Europe,
and the well as much a receptacle of guilt
as the cathedral's font. And consider the potential,
no, consider the necessity, of a flaxen-haired girl
merging in this field of vision and then erupting
from a point above the waterline, the tree stump.

Skippy Rock, Augusta: Warning, the undertow

1

Oyster catchers
scout the tight rutilic
beach rust charting

run-off locked
cross-rock up-coast
from the bolted

lighthouse
where two oceans
surge & rip & meet.

2

Immense the deep lift
seizes in gnarls & sweeps,
straight up & built

of granite. A black
lizard rounds & snorts
the froth capillaried

up towards dry-land's
limestone, hill-side
bone marrow mapped

by water. Meta-wrought,
the lighthouse distantly
elevates & turns

the crazily
bobbing history
of freak waves

and wrecks: wrought-iron
& lead paint brewing
deep in capsized

sealanes, talking shop
in thick clots of language,
bubbles thundering topwards.

3
The stab-holes
of fishing poles,
small-boy whipping

boy those gate-
crashing waves releasing
shoals of wrecked

cuttlefish bleeding sepia
like swell prising
the weed-swabbed rocks

& darkly crescented beach:
crabclaw & limpet
scuttlebut

about the rubbery
swathes of kelp.
Tenebrous lash

& filigreed canopy
of dusk-spray, undertow
of night.

Chilli Catharsis

It fortifies my blood
against the heat
of separation—
a placebo.
Fire against fire.
Unleash your black
lightning: anti-sex,
space condensed ultra
or even collapsed.
I take I take.
This the poet
abusing language
for the sake of stasis—
the symbol as solid
as you wish. The devil's tool,
the devil's number.
Concrete. The sculpted
chilli. Like falling
on your own sword.
The heat the heat.
Fall into my burnt body
and torch your anger,
a chilli dance
for our son—fantasia
purified. Clean
but cold. Our sweat ice
on swollen cheeks. Chillies
charred at our feet.

On Entering Your Thirty-First Year

ref. Byron, Porter, Tranter et al.

The saturation of your art
despite trying to live outside your poetry
as ART yells harshly, 'It's just you
                trying hard to get out!'—

too exciting by half, the question is what to do (with)
this excess energy that seems to be
the signature—de rigueur—of the Age,
                or even *recherché?*

That you or they are satisfied with the echo
of the Master naming Names that might well
include your own, or in the very least, the name of some-
                one you could claim to 'know'

but unfortunately stuck with habits
no one wants to own, like keeping those mull
plants (stuck wanly on your sunless balcony,
                withering impolitely),

or going clothesless in the kitchen, 'wander-
lust' a catastrophe just waiting to happen:
the river coolly photogenic
                and too much like a line waiting to be

snorted. Unlike the discotheque's sullen
attraction, which is the animal in the
poem waiting to get out—though the phone
                brings the party to you.

But look, at thirty this is seen as keeping
it reasonably under control:
and as long as the lines keep writing themselves—
              which they don't—you won't need pay

for therapy or attend glum AA meetings.
Hey, scratch your meanings on a brown paper bag
that's been chock-a-block with nuts and cans
              and that will do for the scholar

or librarian: those nagging voices so strongly
coming on, that to avoid your avid Nature is danger—
calenture and betrayal of the facts,
              that nothing can trouble words

(roughly translated as the joy of life, just for you)—
the music not a scratch on Thrash or Goth
or even *The Magic Flute*, *Messiah*,
              or Iggy Pop's 'Passenger.'

And money as imitation takes
liberties or dupes you into thinking that a nice bloke would
always give away his room to strangers
              and simultaneously con

a few grand out of his mother. Metrical
consistency is a poor excuse,
but things like this only show themselves with distance—
              the ear having nothing

to do with pissing yourself in public,
delirium tremens, or a solid
dose of pox to keep the machine on its toes;
              rather, a need to peruse

or be perused by almost perfect words
in almost perfect order—this comes
as a politically correct excuse
                    near as I can guess.

That only your lust for social
failure (raison d'être?) will drive
you beyond the abyss towards a spiritual bliss,
                    howling to the Feds,

as the Age will hopefully decree, some day:
these were inaugural signs of decay,
that worse was yet to come: music, painting,
                    and words as ART—per verse!

Warhol at Wheatlands

He's polite looking over the Polaroids
saying gee & fantastic, though always
standing close to the warm glow

of the Wonderheat as the flames
lick the self-cleansing glass.
It's winter down here & the sudden

change has left him wanting. Fog
creeps up from the gullies & toupées
the thinly pastured soil. It doesn't

remind him of America at all. But there's
a show on television about New York so
we stare silently, maybe he's asleep

behind his dark glasses? Wish Tom
& Nicole were here. He likes the laser
prints of Venice cluttering the hallway,

the sun a luminous patch trying
to break through the dank cotton air
& the security film on the windows.

Deadlocks & hardened glass make him feel
comfortable, though being locked inside
with Winchester rifles has him tinfoiling

his bedroom—he asks one of us but we're
getting ready for seeding & can't spare a moment.
Ringnecked parrots sit in the fruit trees

& he asks if *they're* famous. But he
doesn't talk much (really). Asked about Marilyn
he shuffles uncomfortably—outside, in the

spaces between parrots & fruit trees
the stubble rots & the day fails
   to sparkle.

The Ascension of Sheep

The sun has dragged
the fog away
and now the sheep
in sodden clothes may

fleece the farmer—
who warm by the fire
tallies heads and prices
and thinks about slaughter—

each soul taken upwards
from its fertile
body—columns of mist
like pillars of a temple.

Come midday they'll
have dried right through
and follow the trail
down to the dam

where the water
refills the empty chamber
where the soul
could never feel secure.

Sculpting a Poem from the Landscape's Painting

'If poetry deals with moral philosophy, painting deals with natural philosophy. Poetry describes the action of the mind, painting considers what the mind may effect by the motions (of the body). If poetry can terrify people by hideous fictions, painting can do as much by depicting the same things in action. Supposing that a poet applies himself to represent beauty, ferocity, or a base, a foul or a monstrous thing, as against a painter, he may in his way bring forth a variety of forms; but will the painter not satisfy more? Are there not pictures to be seen, so like the actual things, that they deceive men and animals?'

—Leonardo da Vinci (*Notebooks*, 654)

1 The Painting

The house yard harbours plumes of rust-faced dock concentrated
            mainly about drainage outlets and depressions left
by reclaimed plough discs. Neglected fruit trees weighed down
not with fruit but lichen stoop over beds of offcut wool which
            in summer will help retain the moisture and prolong
            their contracting lives. Fallen fences, powerlines
from an abandoned generator shed that tether jeans and shirts
of double thickness—it falls below zero most winter mornings.

Following the tilt of the land brings you to the creek. Years
            back the usurping farmers cut the throats of wandoo
and blackbutt, redgum and shaggy-headed dryandra bushes. The
water flows rapidly now, carrying a frothing head of salt over
            granite falls. Then moving uphill and northwards
            you come to the door of the forest, uneasy on its
broken hinges. A spent shotgun cartridge sits on its shod foot,
detonator dark and gaping towards a sky black and swollen.

A ridge within the forest: gravel fluid against the glacial
           granite, collecting in tea-tree smothered clefts
and creases, moraines. Burnt flower heads shed by dryandra
bushes neatly cradle the mummified corpses of gnats and bees,
           while relatives fan their wings busily high in the
           damp hair of wandoo. Overhead a Piper Cherokee wanders
in and out of the clouds as if trying to avoid the most savage
breakers on a turbulent, bitter sea. A hawk dives predictably.

Deeper now. At times the flora tightly bound. But still evidence
           of the sleeper cutters who cut and dragged, chained
massive trunks to bullocks and ripped them from the forest. Jam
           trees and box poison surround deserted adzes, chips
           of wood dulling grey. Heart-leaf and runner poison,
spotted gums peeling and dressing granite boulders, kangaroos
disturbing a pair of western rosellas. Boodie-rat warrens bloat

and bubble skywards, empty now, decimated by the red fox. Black
           cockatoos harvest dryandra blossom by nipping the base
of the flower heads. An echidna curls tightly in the niche at
the base of a naked spotted gum. A copse of sheoaks beckons
           and you've gone full circle, back to the tilting
           edge. A brown owl sits stiffly and winks slowly
as you paint observation into landscape. Sheep drench containers
nestled amongst coils of wire, the broken bodies of tractors.

2 *The Poem*
           A room that is poorly lit apart from a fire spitting
in the grate. Something reminds you that 'Jam country is lowest
           and the first to go with salt.' Is it true? Have
           you never seen a jam tree on a hill or surviving
where the land is salty? Should an idle thought project you from
the room and into the yard, and then northwards up the slope,

across the paddock and into the forest in search
of evidence to support this rumour? No, it is cold

outdoors, and you've spent enough time in the forest
to scan your memory and produce an answer. Surely. In closing
        your eyes you develop a picture, and from this
        picture words should flow, mingle with song—
the sound of a black cockatoo shrieking to its mate or a fox
risking the daylight to scream its song most often reserved
        for the depths of night. But from this comes a
        mass of contradictions: donkey orchids flowering

out of season, echidnas climbing spotted gums
to reclothe them with the latest fashion, sheep drench drums
        making the forest verdant. Snap out of it, return
        to the room—ideas that sing should not be fused
with words if sanity is to be preserved. Instead, paint pictures
and distil a moral truth from this. Poetry will not tolerate
        a mix of concept and the visual, it fools neither
        forest creature nor human.

3 Envoi
It is summer now and the water in the dams is diminishing.
Koonak and marron shells mark water's rank retreat. The forest
        is dry and volatile. The dock with its rust has
dried and vanished. The paddocks are dust. A would-be aesthete

you sift the platitudes of seasonal change. You search out
a painting to compare this image before you with that of winter.
        The painting is vivid though lifeless. On its back:
        'Jam country is the lowest and the first to go with salt.'

Rock Picking: Building Cairns

The spine is best kept straight—
the weight of granite will damage
vertebrae, stretch the spinal cord.
   Let the knees do the work,
legs levering the load from ground
to trailer dragged at a crawl behind
      the Massey Ferguson tractor.

Cairnwards we move over the paddock,
building these self-contained environments
for snakes, spiders, and bush-wise architects.
   Ground lost is ground gained,
these cairns are completely functional.
Satellite cities linked by machinery that's
      commuter friendly if unpredictable.

Rune stones carefully placed, oblatory,
offerings for local deaths—accidents at harvest,
on gravel roads, wild tractor's overturning,
augers catching a hand and swallowing flesh.
   And deities only farmers know.

Dried lichen and sweat mix to cement a cairn.
The surface suppressing the glitter of quartz—
pink, rose, white, transparent. Sources of warmth
these repositories of micro-chip technology
(unharnessed) attract infra-red telescopics,
blood coursing through their Frankenstein

monster bodies, distracting the predator's weapon
as it roams in search of foxes and rabbits.
Cairns—where youths empty swollen bladders
drunkenly into the fissures and cast amber bottles
into cobwebbed abysses, where wild oats grow at
impossible angles and lure the sun into darkness.

As I rock pick I unravel these pictures and spread
them to all corners of the paddock. I coin phrases,
devise anecdotes, invest the ups and downs of my
life in these cairns constructed from the landscape's
    wreckage, place sheep skulls on summits.

Alone, I feed these rowdy cities the stuff
of my blisters, sign the structures with broken
fingers, convert plans to ash and scatter
    them about the foundations.
Softly softly I sing the ruins of our
pampered anatomies, draw strength from the
    harsh realities of empire building.

And following duskfall, the tractor
and trailer no longer visible, I climb
onto the motorbike and drape myself over
    the seat—a bag of bones
slung over the tray of an iron jinker.
As the tractor comes into focus the cairns
    retreat—pyramids of the outback.

Poem for Those at Wheatlands

You only realise
that the stars
over the low
fluorescent crops
are particular
to the frame
of Wheatlands,
that the canvas
stretched
against the salt
is a photo-
sensitive plate
that might take
generations
to expose
(below, another waits!).
And that family
ashes
are the size
that will hold
souls, stars, and soil
in place.

The Silo

Visitors, as if they knew, never remarked
on the old silo with its rammed earth walls
and high thatched roof, incongruous amongst
the new machinery and silver field bins.
Nor the workers brought in at harvest time,
trucks rolling past the ghostly whimperings,
snarls and sharp howls cutting the thick silo's
baffling. Nor when a bumper harvest filled
every bin and the farmer was hungry
for space—no one ever mentioned bringing
the old silo back into service. This
had been the way for as far back as could
be remembered. Thin sprays of baby's breath
grew around its foundations, while wedding
bouquet sprouted bizarrely from the grey
mat of thatching. The sun had bleached the walls
bone-white while the path to the heavily
bolted door was of red earth, a long thin
stream of unhealthy blood. Before those storms
which brew thickly on summer evenings
red-tailed black cockatoos settled in waves,
sparking the straw like a volcano, dark
fire erupting from the heart of the white
silo, trembling with energy deeper
than any anchorage earth could offer.
And lightning dragging a moon's bleak halo
to dampen the eruption, with thunder
echoing out over the bare paddocks
towards the farmhouse where an old farmer

consoled his bitter wife on the fly-proof
verandah, cursing the cockatoos, hands
describing a prison from which neither
could hope for parole, petition, release.

Why They Stripped the Last Trees from the Banks of the Creek

They stripped the last trees
from the banks of this creek
twenty years ago. The old man
couldn't stand the thought
of bare paddocks with a creek
covered by trees slap bang
in the middle of them.
A kind of guilt I guess.
Anyway, he was old
and we humoured him—
chains, rabbit rippers,
chainsaws. We cleared
those banks until the water
ran a stale sort of red.
Until salt crept into
the surrounding soaks.
Furious he was—the salt
left lines on the bath,
the soap wouldn't lather.

Fog

For all its lymphatic nature
fog appears rapidly and spreads
its shroud tightly about the farm.

And though blinding, sheep and people
stumble smoothly through its unguent
body. Wood smoke fails to coerce

its opacity and drops moistly.
Apparently sectile it flinches
though heals instantly.

You drink its flesh with every breath.
Settling on low grounds it climbs
to the peaks of hills and spills,

using trees and granite outcrops
as hungry boards. A submariner,
I walk the ocean's floor.

The fog thickens about the family
graves, tarnishing plaques
and chilling icons to the bone.

Finches zip like apparitions,
the sun, a limp beacon, drifts
to the rim of the system.

I mark the blurred silver
of a galvanised tank
as a point for navigation

and set off through the red flesh
of failing saltbush, over a carpet
of mustard sheoak needles.

The ground sinks and thickens.
In this quasi-world I hesitate—
as the fog burns my skin I sense

a fire's shadow and hear water
crackling as it fuels the mass
of liquid flame. A living entity

the fog accepts me—I move steadily
on, confident that I will emerge
without a mark on my body.

Goading Storms Out of a Darkening Field

Goading storms out of a darkening field,
Cockeyed bobs seeding the salt, the farmer
Cursing the dry, cursing the bitter yield.

And while lightning would savage him with skilled
Thrusts, and floods strip the topsoil, it's better
Goading storms out of a darkening field

Than sit distraught on the verandah, killed
By the 'quitter's syndrome'—it's much safer
Cursing the dry, cursing the bitter yield.

Field bins empty, coffers bare, should have sold
Two years back when prices were halfway there.
Goading storms out of a darkening field.

Red harvest, charred hills, dry wells filled and sealed.
Sheep on their last legs. Dams crusted over.
Cursing the dry, cursing the bitter yield.

It's tempting when prayers and patience have failed,
Diviners have lost track of ground water.
Goading storms out of a darkening field.
Cursing the dry, cursing the bitter yield.

Parrot Deaths: Rites of Passage

Blue clouds scuttle the eucalypt sun
as it fizzes and winces with impending
rain, sultry weather dampening
the orange hearts of king parrots.

The scimitar roads cull the golden grain
from dump trucks and belly spillers, tarps
tethered loosely, illegal loads shifting
over axles tense with excess tonnage.

Rosellas gather about the grain offerings
and the torn bodies of the fallen. Wood smoke
hustles a magpie lark out of an uncharacteristic
torpor. A crow hangs low and watches intently.

Observing the rites of passage a regent
parrot plunges into the dead eyes of a semi,
eyes of silver nitrate, tarnished and stained
shadow black. The orange, golden, and emerald

hearts of parrots litter the roads. I drive
slowly and whisper prayers of deflection.

Skeleton weed/generative grammar

(i) Finite-state
The 'i' takes in what is said—
yes, it is easily led
across the floors of discourse
only to find itself a force
easily reckoned with: there's
no point in stock-taking arrears
as fleshly interests tell you
nothing except acceptability & taboo.
Take skeleton weed infesting
the crop—rosette of basal
leaves unleashing a fatal
stem with *daisy-like* flowers
that drop (into) parachute clusters
of seeds. One missed when
they scour the field (men
& women anonymously-clothed
seated on a spidery raft dragged
behind a plodding tractor,
monotony testing the free-will factor),
can lead to disaster.

(ii) Phrase-structure
{[(((analyz)ing)] [the ((constituent)s)]}
we examine(?) the wool of sheep
for free-loading skeleton-weed seeds,
their teeth specifically designed
for wool: the ag department
have decided they ARE selective
though admit our investigations
will help their 'research'.

(iii) transformational

One year the farmer asked us if we
felt guilty for missing one & hence ruining
his would-have-been bumper crop.
Quarantined the following year. Losing
his unseeded would-be bumper crop.
Ruining his credit rating. His marriage.
His son's & daughter's places
at their exclusive city boarding
schools. His problem with alcohol.
His subsequent breakdown
& hospitalization. (?) We remained
& still remain passive. Still we remained
& remain passive. But we [look(ed)] deeply,
collectively & independently
into our SELVES. Our silence
was an utterance of a loud inner speech.
A loud inner speech was an utterance
of our silence. Speaking for myself,
I've included in my lexicon of guilt
the following: what I feel today
will I feel tomorrow? And those tight
yellow flowers: so beautiful on the wiry
structures they call 'skeleton weed.'

Bluff Knoll Sublimity

for Tracy

1.

The dash to the peak anaesthetizes
you to the danger of slipping as the clouds
in their myriad guises wallow about
the summit. The rocks & ground-cover
footnotes to the sublime. The moods
of the mountain are not human
though pathetic fallacy is the surest
climber, always willing
to conquer the snake-breath
of the wind cutting over
the polished rockface,
needling its way through taut
vocal cords of scrub.

2.

It's the who you've left behind
that becomes the concern as distance
is vertical and therefore less inclined
to impress itself as separation; it's as if you're
just hovering in the patriarchy
of a mountain, surveying
the tourists—specks on the path
below. Weather shifts are part of this
and the cut of sun at lower altitudes
is as forgiving as the stripped
plains, refreshingly green at this time
of year. You have to climb it because it's
'the highest peak' in this flat state,

and the 'you have to' is all you
can take with you as statement
against comfort and complacency:
it's the vulnerability that counts up here.

3.
You realise that going there to write a poem
is not going there at all, that it's simply
a matter of embellishment, adding
decorations like altitude,
validating a so so idea
with the nitty gritty of conquest.
Within the mountain another
body evolves—an alternate
centre of gravity holding
you close to its face.
From the peak you discover
that power is a thick, disorientating
cloud impaled by obsession, that
on seeing Mont Blanc—THE POEM—
and not Mont Blanc—THE MOUNTAIN—
the surrounding plains
with their finely etched topography
can be brought into focus.

Of Writing at Wheatlands

"a small bird's frightened feather"

1.
Asked about the wandoo
and what it signifies: the spirit,
hollowing trees struck and cast
as didgeridoos, the ghosts
of a burnt yellow landscape
gloating over aneurisms
in the waspish air,
and the redgum, blood of the earth,
clustering thickly on the lower ground,
staining Arcadia with its brutish sap.
And the magpie lark reversing
into the path of a charging car
as stooks render patronizing
the effete comments of continuance,
as the oppressed, the insignificant,
glow rewardingly in successful
forecast, a longing increased
with the familiar patterns
of recall: the death of the crop,
the harvest, the errant blue wren
defying geographies, as if an idyll
is possible, while downwind a trail
of devastated pink and grey galahs
destroys the imagery, the sky's
many bands of film,
each with its different
and untruthful qualities,
the drill bit biting deep
into chalky dirt, dry

is *recherché*, is the notional exile
you impose upon yourself
as if you have a choice.

2.
a small bird's frightened feather
informs the screen and lustrous
is the Kodachrome of labour,
the sweat on the bare backs
of the worker, the occasional
smile out of context, and home
they go well satisfied they've
seen it as it is, the bird
somewhere else: plummeting

3. the translations are absorbed: organically
stones skipping across the dam
in the tonal languages
of investment, it's what
you can't give up

of not rendering something that has intrinsic beauty
into something that would acquire beauty

would you stop denying
and in those moments
reach for a similar idyllicism?

4. the space traversed
It's as if you want to anoint
this place again,
as if you had this place
despite its fences

: to lay the gridwork
over the particulars as value
<u>should</u> be added with imperial
measurement

like duration,
the clot of sand re-welded
in every incantation,
the frozen framework
of title deeds in a place
so hot the salt looks cold enough
to weld touch to its glittering surface,

though seasonal change
retains always the essence of <u>the</u>

as we en-DUR{ATION}
measure against our spatial
configuration

5. A Letter Written in Earlier Life to Your Future Wife
Prep land for seeding
in late night fox ochre
and Deleuze in the spotlight
having none of its flamboyance
in the moment of concentrated
undertaking, the collaboration
of disk and moisture
after the first rains,
and the dragging of an exploiting
culture across the bones
and viscous remains of:
the red bark the fox of the one wheel in line

introducing the thud of pistons and sounds
in clay churned as clods,
the *boondies* of childhood
like stolen nouns
beneath the local transfer
that beyond the cramped conditions
in the tractor's cabin
there is always conveyance
of another nature:
a darkly changing aspect

Anathalamion

My parents dead & the family property
broken up, I live on *their* place—in the old shearing
quarters—& keep an eye on things. Talking
business with the old man is impossible though the old lady
comes to the quarters once a week & we sit with a cuppa & study
the week's takings—sorting out the bills & tallying
the red & black figures. She's always been good
with numbers. But it's like she's given up caring
about things really—just working the sums to trade
away the bad memories. The old man sits in a hide
down by the creek some days—watching the blue heron
high in the redgum tree that was blasted
by lightning years back. When I go to the hotel
they ask me what the old couple do these days but I just get plastered
& stare into my beer—snubbing even the mayor—'to Hell
with the lot of you!' I'll yell, just waiting for a quarrel.
On a dark day, when the season was closing in,
they were seen leaving the town, like the blue heron.

After their son's death the blue heron became the old man's obsession
and his wife told me he only ever spoke to her when talking of them.
The blue heron, their nest raided by crows, have left the redgum this year.
I like to think they're nesting nearby—maybe further upcreek where the
redgums are still thick. Their son had once claimed that he'd been told
by a hay stooker that if you died near a heron your soul joined with its
soul. He'd told that to his parents and they'd laughed. He marvelled
that it was called a blue heron when it was more of a grey colour. On a
dark day, when the season was closing in, they were seen leaving the town,
like the blue heron.

As children we'd burrow into the hay
or move bales like building blocks, trapping
carpet snakes. Together saw Tad Hunter clutching
at the mangled stump of his arm, the auger crazy
with his blood. Once we nearly drowned in a silo of barley,
sinking further with every move, pulled out crying
by his old man who said we'd learnt our lesson & didn't need
punishing any further. Who said the same, when—riding
his motorbike—we hit the cattle grid & skewed
into the creek. And when we fed a pet sheep his premium seed
wheat & watched it die from pickle poisoning. Neighbours
called us feral kids—'little bastards, getting their claws
into everythin', like locusts in the crop, nothin' can stop
'em.' It's true, we ran amok, but we did our chores
& didn't mean any harm—a chip
off the ol' block his dad would say to the town cop.
On a dark day, when the season was closing in,
they were seen leaving the town, married again.

In some ways it was like a world under glass—porous glass that let in the
creek and the birds and the weather and the children who'd creep up to
the house as a dare, the old people having *that* reputation for strange-
ness, but kept the pain in, petrified in the moment. The boy's death had
cut it off from the outside world and it existed in a twilight which not
even the most determined seasons could breach. I never said much about
him. I read a lot and kept to myself. But even the brightest books seemed
dull. The shadows of the blue heron indelible on their pages. On a dark
day, when the season was closing in, they were seen leaving the town,
like the blue heron.

It was one of those days when the black
cockatoos were low-loping in a storm-stained sky
& the creek ran river-thick, scouring the red clay
banks & swamping the nests of water rats, & the track
up to the top gate was up to the axles with mud & a long trek
around the flooded paddocks was necessary, stray
sheep stuck firm, the silos damp & full of sprouted wheat,
that they both emerged in black raincoats & doggedly
made their way to town on foot. As word had spread, the main street
was lined with adults & children who thought they were in for a treat.
But the old couple didn't lift their heads, & neither led
the other as they marched like mourners or a parody of the dead,
marching a slow funereal slog towards the empty church.
A few moments later the priest appeared
& followed them into the silence beyond the arch.
On a dark day when the season was closing in,
they were seen leaving the town, married again.

Note: 'blue heron' is a local nickname for the 'white-faced
heron'—a bird that is largely blue-grey.

Lightning Tree

It's stark white in this hard
winter light. At its base
brackish water spreads like exposed film
out through marshgrass & paperbarks—
a snapped bone, it punctures the skin.
On its splintered crown
the Great Egret stretches, its knifed beak
piercing the cold blue sky—
an inverted lightning strike
fielding its wings—
a crucifix—hesitating,
as if held by a magnet,
then dropping into flight,
dragging lightning rod legs.

Approaching the Anniversary of my Last Meeting with my Son

I never write 'confessional' poetry
but your voice—like forked lightning
etching a thunder-dark river—leaves me
no choice but to speak directly.
I hear your mother laugh.
That I've screened myself
in the ash of burnt images,
left nothing intact behind.
It's almost the anniversary
of my leaving, and you don't
know my voice on the phone
when you ring Nanna.
Told it's Daddy,
you say, 'I'd better go,'
your mother erupting
from another room;
it's not safe using the phone
during a storm. And peace
is as important at home
as food and warmth, so I let it go.
Sometimes I sit on Deep Water Point jetty
and remember the time we spent
considering what lies below
the glistening surface,
what drives mottled brown jellyfish
in scattered flotillas
to beach themselves,

why herons strut their stuff
curious yet suspicious—
having to answer to no more
than the weather,
small fish, and an urge to be free.

Grave

Serpentine. Tracy asks me to stop
at the cemetery—her brother
who drowned in Wungong Dam
is buried here. She clears
dry leaves from the framed
blue metal while I think
of Craig whose grave
I've never visited.
It's just something I can't face.
Though I'll wander almost happily
amongst the tombs of those I've
not known. I did not know
Tracy's brother, and it shows.
I set out in search of flowers.
It is autumn and they are scarce.
Behind the cemetery I come across
lines of dead sheep. Wool, red
with raddle paint, hangs
dankly about the carcasses.
I return empty handed.
One can't transfer flowers
from another's grave.
At the right time of year
Tracy says kangaroo paws
are rampant—occasionally
erupting from graves,
bloody windchimes
muttering under their breaths.

Tenebrae

for Tracy

You are on the verge
of a resurrection,
standing on a fragile shoreline,
erosion undermining
the limestone cliff face,
expecting to plunge suddenly
into the churning ocean.
You'd rebuild memories,
though this coastline
is always changing—a childhood
hiding place eroded,
an overhang collapsed
like the tide. Those
limestone columns
reaching towards a god
that would take your past
as if it were an offering.
But though the lights
one by one extinguish
as you explore deeper,
that final light—the sun—
grows stronger,
despite the coming winter,
the darkening seas.

Solitary Activities

'He spent his working hours deflating words
and every Saturday he spied on birds.'
      'Mars Sonnet No 5'—Peter Porter

Poetry is not the only thing
That you can 'do' alone in a room;
You could, like Andrew Crosse,
Imagine living creatures
Created by electrical currents
                              passing
Through brilliant chemical mixtures
The colour of tropical birds.
                        Or believe
That Morley Martin, alone in *his* room,
Produced 'primordial protoplasm'
From fossil-free Azoic Rock;
                              but that's what
Comes with reading dictionaries
Of Common Fallacies and being alone
Yourself—the weekday air thick with words,
The weekend call of birds a long way off.

Wild Radishes

Across the dark fields the family is spread
While overhead the sky is haunted,
In the dull light they scour the crop
Never looking up as the day seems to stop.
Wild radishes missed will destroy the yield—
Bills to be paid, deals to be sealed.
But the plover's refusal to lift and drop,

And the absence of crow and parrot talk,
And the immense racket as stalk rubs on stalk,
Registers somewhere deep in the soul.
And as the sun begins to uncoil—
The deep green of the wheat uneasy with light—
The golden flowers of wild radishes bite
Just before they are ripped from the soil.

Drowning in Wheat

They'd been warned
on every farm
that playing
in the silos
would lead to death.
You sink in wheat.
Slowly. And the more
you struggle the worse it gets.
'You'll see a rat sail past
your face, nimble on its turf,
and then you'll disappear.'
In there, hard work
has no reward.
So it became a kind of test
to see how far they could sink
without needing a rope
to help them out.
But in the midst of play
rituals miss a beat—like both
leaping in to resolve
an argument
as to who'd go first
and forgetting
to attach the rope.
Up to the waist
and afraid to move.
That even a call for help
would see the wheat
trickle down.
The painful consolation
of time. The grains

in the hourglass
grotesquely swollen.
And that acrid
chemical smell
of treated wheat
coaxing them into
a near-dead sleep.

The Hunt

for Les Murray

A bounty of 'fame throughout the district and no
chores for a week' was placed on The Tiger by my
        Uncle. We'd all seen it
        plenty of times over
the years—a huge beast that came down from the Top Bush
and raided the chicken coop, took the guinea fowl,
        and slaughtered pets. It was
a true feral, begotten by ferals. It was,

in a sense, a species entire in itself.
Those many sightings over the years of a 'large
        predator' we put down
        to The Tiger. It seemed
like a joke of nature—green-grey fur with musty
yellow waves running like stripes down its flanks, massive
        jaw with steel teeth that shone
as it snarled in a spotlight before vanishing

into the bush. For two years it had been hunted—
even the local pro fox shooter couldn't bring
        home its scalp. One winter
        holidays my cousin
and I packed our tent and kit, shouldered arms and crossed
into the scrub. Deep into the dark forbidding
        foliage we plunged. We struck
        camp close to the centre
of the island of wandoo and mallee, a large

copse surrounded by florescent green crops of wheat.
At dusk we shot three grey rabbits as they emerged
        from their warrens. It was
        quick and nothing was said.
Placing them in a damp hessian sack we spent hours
traipsing through the bush by torchlight, dragging the sack
        behind us. The scent spread,
        we emptied the corpses
on a patch of open ground and set to digging

hollows and laying traps—fierce iron jaws decayed
by rust, straining beneath sand-covered newspaper
        disguising the ambush.
        We took turns in laying
them, one holding the torch, the other spiking chains
into dirt, bracing springs with a boot. The traps ringed
        the offering. Rubbing
the ground with a corpse we masked our sharp scent before

casting it back on the pile. The cold bit at our
bones. Finished, we didn't linger—a strange fear took
        hold of us and something
        nudged its way under our
confidence. We returned to the campsite. Morning
was bitter—tamarisks were heavy with frost, sheathed
        with rapiers of ice.
        We struggled with a fire,
ate by the smouldering, eye-stinging hearth. Rifles

in hand we made our way to the place. *The Altar
of the Dead* one of us muttered without humour.
        The Tiger was there. Dead—
        frozen solid. The stripes

on its flanks blurred by the dark matting of fur. Three
of the traps had snatched its limbs; the others had been
       triggered and lay beaten
nearby. The Tiger had chewed off its trapped forepaw

which lay half-digested in the trap's maw, back legs
stretched as if by some medieval torturing
       device. The carcasses
       of the rabbits had not
been touched. We buried them with The Tiger; buried
the traps, deep. We packed our gear and went home, telling
       Uncle that The Tiger
       would never be caught, that
it was a creature not of this world—a bitter
cold had struck our bones, fire bringing no relief.

An Aerial View of Wheatlands
in Mid-Autumn

'Indeed, it is a question if the exclusive reign of this orthodox beauty
is not approaching its last quarter.'
—Thomas Hardy, *The Return of the Native*

In the reciprocity of summer
And the year's first frosts, the green eruption
Hesitant, the stramineous remainder
Of last season's crop converts to nitrogen
As slowly overhead the spotter plane
Dissects the quickening flesh of Wheatlands,
The probing eye of the camera hidden
From your curious surveillance, while stands
Of mallee gnaw at the salty badlands.

They will offer to sell you the stolen
Moment, the frozen minutiae of your
Movement within the tableau, the tension
Extracted with such unwanted exposure:
The screams of the cockatoo, the tractor
Aching deep in its gut having swallowed
A brace of teeth as it crunched into gear,
Bleats of sheep on their way to be slaughtered,
The drift as a neighbour sprays weedicide.

Remember though that if given the chance
You would scrutinize someone else's yard,
So it may be worth adjusting your stance
In the light of such a double standard.
Forget that the land looks scarred and tortured:
That call for order in the rural scene,

For Virgil's countryside satiated
With weighty corn and Campanian wine,
And consumed by olives and wealthy swine,

Is not the harmony of this decade.
Instead look to the flux of soil and fire,
The low-loping flight of the darkest bird,
The frantic dash of the land-bound plover,
The breaking of salt by errant samphire,
The flow of water after steady rain,
The everlasting in bright disorder,
The stealthy path of the predating plane
Cutting boundaries as you sow your grain.

The Machine of the Twentieth Century Rolls Through the High-Yielding Crop

Dust particles cling to sweat despite the sun just up,
moisture levels within brittle stalks drop
as rapidly as markets are lost or gained, shadow
puppetry of information exchange leading the finest
of mechanical technologies astray, as over the crop

the machine of the twentieth century poises—straining
against dry dock, a Titanic that won't be sunk in those deepest
spots of abundance, a post-modern Ceres busy at the helm
lest a hidden rock break the fingers clawing in the grain;
this schizophrenic God whose speech is a rustle, a token bristling

like static on the stereo, despite state-of-the-art electronics
and a bathyspherical cabin of glass and plastic sealed
against all intrusion though retaining hawk-like vision and radio
contact with the outside world. On the fringes—at home base,
or by the gate—the workers are ready to launch out, to drain

grain from a bulging bin. The art of harvesting is in the hiding
of the operation. Behind clean lines and sun-deflecting paint
the guts of the machine work furiously; from point of entry
to expulsion the process is relentless—from comb working greedily,
grain spirals up elevators, thrashed in a drum

at tremendous speeds, straw spewed out back by
manic straw-walkers, the kernels falling to sieves below
as fans drive cocky chaff out into the viscous
daylight. The sun at mid-morning rages out of control,
glutted on this excess fuel. Melanomas spread on field workers

as they tarp a load; the driver plunges with precision
back into the crop, setting a perfect line, de-mystifying
this inland sea—an illusion, a mirage that hangs around
just before summer has reached full-blown. City granaries
filling, factories churning, 'design' a catchword instigating

plenty—the risks of intensive farming, tomorrow's worry—
stubble itching, high yields floating like oil on troubled waters,
the Titanic's myth attracting the districts of the hungry.

Skylab and The Theory of Forms

for Jeremy Prynne

We didn't make it but we ended up getting it,
or parts of it at least. I've seen chunks
and my wife's father brought some home
for them as kids. In the tradition
of those splinters of the True Cross
held in reliquaries around the world,
if you added all the chunks
together there'd have been an entire
city in space. There's a novel simmering
in its iconic resonance, the charred black
remains the talisman that starts
or in the very least attracts a cult.
Like the Aum Supreme Truth Cult,
that had a place out there, somewhere
where the land is less fertile and not so
closely scrutinised. Members may
not have known about Skylab
but the prospect of the world
crashing down on their neighbours
would have spurred them on.
But Skylab's not like them,
nor like the couple from the Subcontinent
who named their newborn in its honour,
being American it's as good as having
Elvis or Marilyn paraphernalia dropped
in your back yard. People pay
good money for stuff like this.
Kids of my generation remember
the diagrams in magazines

and newspapers. The neat bodies
of astronauts suspended in the neat
compartments. Small had great potential.
And it looked much more modern
than anything the Ruskies
could put up there. But maybe now
we can see that such assumptions
were merely a matter of taste.
Soviet Space Trash is also
worth a fortune, and promises
the exotic in the subtext
of THE modern novel. A kind of
accidental empire building,
an occupation of the vacant spaces.
Like Woomera. A roar that fills
the void of Terra Nullius.

The Bermuda Triangle

Pat Rafter, saviour of Australian tennis,
maintains a comfortable existence on Bermuda;
the flight of balls determined by the weather
which island-culture makes more tropical
than it should—the concentration of emptiness
and expectation like nationalism postponed
and sent offshore—the Queen's English
an experimental turn of phrase on the front
doorstep of liberty, the fraternal vanishings
of flight on flight of the right stuff, as if Play-
Station IS living, as if a package holiday
has you hungering after the wealth
of the pyramids, concentrated to an echoing
point of ambiguity, like the limitations
of radar, and re-runs of *The Day the Earth
Stood Still*—remaining black and white
as childhood—making an ocean of the river,
the bright ship whispering through the ever
widening hole in the ozone layer.

The Road to Brookton—*on the nature of memory*

for John Kerrigan

Back from England and fenland
we drive into the wheatbelt—
warm weather with the possibility
of a storm late in the day.
Or maybe it is cool, but warm
when compared with where
we've come from. Breaching
the Hills reservoirs and quarries
that feed the city, the excursion
reconstructs itself: everlastings
thick on roadsides broadcast
ethnographies and genealogies,
preparing for their seed-drop—
a dried persistent thought withering
and flaking like insect wings,
blown into the cautiously drying crop,
awaiting reconstitution. Movement
plays like a home video. Crops
and road-killed animals compile
as data—memory a webcrawler
hyperventilating references:
the yield looks okay from here,
that roo is still alive, gasping
for its last breath on the road's
gravel shoulder. There's gelatine
in this Kodak film, the sky's
too bright—glistens and gleams
like a cibachrome print.
They imported convict labour

late in the picture. Land rights
are up against it around here.
This State voted for secession
in the thirties. Was this one
of the roads resurfaced
with a Federal grant
during the Bicentennial Year?
A landmark defines itself—
granite outcrop or gnarled tree
in a very flat field fringed
by firebreaks. A UFO
was spotted hovering
over a field of gamenya wheat
last year. That's what we heard.
A little to the west the face
of Christ made an appearance
on a slab of stone—looking
mediaeval and European.
In a letter, on the telephone.
A scrap of gossip loose in memory.
It was, well . . . whatever.
Old technology. The new model
goes quickly out of date.
General Motors, Ford, Nissan.
I was reading Kropotkin
and thinking about Sidney Nolan.
We pass a beer can, a bullet-ridden
milepost, a broken fan-belt.
Radio waves lasso the culture.
The bright renderings—tarps on field bins,
on truck trailers—glow authentically
and we all have our say.
It's true, there's a waterbird
on the edge of the scrub

eating carrion. Dead sheep or roo.
It's the recollection that reeks.
It seemed logical at the time.
As if it had come to this, or that.
Between the properties Crown land
sticks out like a sore thumb.
The shells of burnt-out cars
confuse spotter planes and satellites.
A total fireban is close.
We listen for the news.
Overtaking, something is missed.
A dam brines beneath
the billowing stratosphere.
Bitumen wavers. Brookton
moves closer. A creek shadows
the highway—unmapped,
so there's hope for dialect.
The locals sleep away
their Sunday. Lightning stirs up
heat and recall grows oppressive.
All tenses and figures of speech
sulphur-crested white cockatoos
lift with Hitchcockian malevolence,
as if they shouldn't be there,
as if placid crows perched
on second-hand farm machinery
and rusted swings under wandoo trees
have conspired and incited them.
Caught out, struck down
by the suddenness of the storm,
we imagine that we're part of it,
that we belong there too,
knowing in the electric air
that this is not true.

After Sir Lawrence Alma-Tadema's 94°
in the Shade (1876)

for Peter Porter

'THYRSIS:
Sit down now, goatherd (think the Nymphs had asked you),
And play your pipe, here where the hillside steepens
And tamarisks grow on the slope. I will watch your goats.'
     —Theocritus, 'Idyll 1'

The country in summer. The temperature hovers
    around the low thirties—
it is something of a heatwave. The surrounding
fields are tawny gold, though green tinges are almost
    tactless within a world
contracted to the killing jar. Unseen birds fuse,
tarnish with a chemical sky. Sullen trees wreck

the view so it's photosensitive. Animals
    twitch beneath the herbage.
Landscape and portrait hang languidly about each
other. In the foreground a youth is spread out cheek-
    in-hand, reading a book
on butterflies. His weapon—the butterfly net—
lies in front of him. He is confident. Maybe

overconfident. He's wearing an ivory
    summer suit with pith hat;
schoolboy on holidays, resting in the still shade,
confident within the granary of empire, wealth
    that keeps home secure.
Butterflies from other spaces congregate. Stooks
have been gathered, but lie in casual disarray.

Hockney's Doll Boy *at the Local Country Women's Association Annual Musical: Wheatbelt, Western Australia*

Opening night. As the curtain lifts
Doll Boy hovers in the wings,
the Town Hall full as the star drifts

centre-stage and in a falsetto sings
to the roar of the crowd—
the CWA already counting the takings

as the chorus of footy stars makes a loud
entry—smeared make-up and wigs,
ill-fitting blouses, the odd shroud-

length dress. A farmer digs
a mate in the ribs—that strapping
girl's my son, the last vestiges

of his reserve dissipating
with the electricity of the occasion.
At interval, the cast is buzzing

with excitement, taking slices of melon
from Doll Boy's chipped green plate,
blowing him kisses, calling him 'Queen'.

You're just not cute enough to rate
a place among us! Doll Boy, eyes
to himself, begins to create

a space apart, beyond the cries
of the crowd, the taste of melon on his lips:
sweet pink crystals bristling like stars,

full and sweet. And he grips
the memory of the vine—intricately
binding the patch near the roses and strips

of everlastings, ripening rapidly,
drinking the dam's muddy water insatiably,
preparing to feed the elect, delicately.

Shoes once shod in a blacksmith's shop

Shoes once shod in a blacksmith's shop
rust on hooves lying on the rough edge
   of a paddock, horse skeletons
mingle with broken hoppers & elevators
& the iron-ringed wheels of surface strippers—
   sprouted grain thick on the
ground, like chemically stimulated hair.

The warped screens of a seed cleaner
buried to the knees in clay and salt, snake their
   way up towards the stunted fruit trees'
low-slung fruit like apodal spirits in a venomous
light—winter at their heels. Inside the shed
   the bellows groan in their frame
of blackbutt & mudbrick, the coals for the fire-

box lie scattered like shoddy talismans,
& the anvil sits glibly, a dead loadstone.

Il faut cultiver notre jardin

Cleared land is a place of weeds,
bee-wings' razored whirr
and a cut trunk hollowed
by white ants—a font
beneath swabs of cloud.

When sunlight cordons
off an area for display,
hill-clefts and ravines
resist, retaining shadow.
Small birds sing and you

don't think of their name,
the air-drag of crows' wings
just overhead. Jam
trees keep their sap
tight beneath the bark.

Late winter warmth
dries cushions of moss,
rapidly brittle and crumbling
around purple sprays
of Paterson's Curse;

onion grass cuts low weather
and twenty-eights are caught
in a pause, a cessation
of dialogue—instruments
poised about the developing fruits

of the creek canopy.
Working their tails, chests
puffed and springing angles
like hearts, claws hooked
as numbers in a code

that won't quite scan:
but neither does God!
A globe-bodied spider
concentrates a poison
that bothers only flies,

mosquitoes, and ants;
the sun intensifies and parrots
are burnt to silhouettes,
a clear night with frost threatens,
plants folding like prayer.

Hectic Red

Quartz sparks randomly
on the pink and white crust
of the salt flats, spread out
beyond the landing,
where bags of grain—
wheat and oats
in plastic and hessian—
lips sewn shut,
packed tight, flexing dust
and dragging their feet
to the edge, are tipped
onto the truck—feed-
grain, filling out
the flat-top, another body sack
waiting to be fed,
from top to bottom,
the sheep hollow-gutted
in the long dry, green-feed
deficient and this
the diminishing stock
of back-up tucker;
the best paddocks
up beyond the salt
all hoofed and bitten,
stray tufts targeted
and levelled,
dry roots crumbling
and dropping to dried-out
stream-beds beneath,
so no new encrustations
of salt emerge back down

in the low places, just the old crust,
pinking off—at night,
the crazy pick-ups
spinning wheels
and throwing headlights,
the bonnets rising and falling
in choppy waves, the light
as unstable as a camera
and the darkness dropping in
like black sacking; bleak rabbits
dashing about,
their blood infra,
the forecast—hectic red.

drought

a lack of water drives you to the well
deep below the burning surface
where unknown wheel animalcules dwell;
a lack of water drives you to the well
to free sheep from drought's death-spell,
to drop a stone from the furnace,
a lack of water drives you to the well
deep below the burning surface

Funeral Oration

for Joyce Heywood

The grave is a gate you send flowers through,
and the pink blossom frosting the northern hemisphere
is, on closer observation, a confluence of species.
There is a scent that's as much about lingering
as leaving, and it's about time the ploughs
were moving down there. The geographical
centre fluctuates while the magnetic centre
remains rock solid. Prayer goes somewhere
and is not lost and expects nothing back.
An old tree—a York gum—oozes sap
like it's something special in this genealogy.
Most of the family is there and words are said
and those who can't attend wait for news of the dead
        as now it is all about memory.

Hölderlin was not Mad

for Tracy and Martin

Prologue
Graffiti the indicative mood
as refugees collate a conscience
and the euro-jets fly intact
overhead, a stiff wind

coming in from the Atlantic:
the *was* or *will be* spun
like constitutional rights—
Sally Joy restive on a shingle beach,

the Tudor rose curve of Deal's
cinque port deflecting the ordnance:
Henry's clean monastic stone
upwind of Hölderlin in his tower,

flagrant and uplifted as spring
conflates forestry and the majesty
of seasons: Swabian fortitude
ousting Jacobin oppression

as in the home of psychiatry
the ethnically cleansed
cling to logos and script:
we speak—Hölderlin was not Mad.

fragment 1
Seasons of matt or gloss
emptied of implication,

waterbirds swimming against the current,
occlusion of hills:
I might take refuge on either bank
but this stay is transitory—
a bright day opens pore-like senses,
unleashing compacted, out of reason

fragment 2
A light bulb ejects and shatters
North, glass embedded deep:
the tower white and light
and people picnic on banks
as others would:
it is always the next day
and dates don't fit autographs—
precision-guided photographs
suggest place is, and the broadsheets
agree—war won in outer quotes,
as current privileges the scarce,
an educated guess, front line
recollection—we are,
we will be

fragment 3
the steps wind down to the Hölderlin House
and I saturate myself in translation: keep out of the Balkans,
MTV, and dynamic equivalence—see, desperate they laugh
and laugh loud: the mongrel company I keep
in a crowded place, standing room only
though Swabian air is fresh and intra-nationalism
lightly acid rain.
                    A protest. A structure.
And a bringing down—this the gloom

dispersed in rivers,
seasons, Hölderlin's room—
autumn necessary in damping down,
art made in summer's success

fragment 4
Disturbing the perfect
glam tower's darkness
in earlier photographs
restoring tainted woodwork,
and satisfactory revolution
fuelled over
Wordsworth's satisfaction:
a flowering anecdote
and a long walk becoming archival
and multilingual:
assonance and tone
rhythm and mood
side-stepping the issue
floorboards glowing
just for the occasion

fragment 5
Home is where Tracy is.

fragment 6 (bright light)
Constantine trans:
'Day! Day! Now the willows can breathe again
Along my streams and drink. The eyes have light . . .'

This day so bright
the split river my divide—
too bright, this waiting

dull suppression and that hopeless
action. Sharp, avid, reminiscent.
Disturbance—dragonfly
cutting waters, understudied
guiltless. I don't take payment.
Damned contract. Nightmare,
bright light.

fragment 7
Octagonal dovecote
in Hölderlin's tower
nine windows draw water and light
at self-same density
as from a pinpoint tip
turret downcurves
in its three-dimensional
aura
            divining curves
and flat bell balance,
body fluids emptied
like electric reactions
without response: church tower,
town centre, municipal spring
at the mayor's grand function,
overcast on overcast
teal green flow
river tracking a brisk jog
slewing moisture and mildew
as the stone of the tower
beneaths a mood
mustard yellow, reflecting
itself, heavy
water, slurry

fragment 8 (indentikit)
sub-fragment (i)

growing up knowing then you are
  and will be when it's convenient
   for them—or anyone—to oppress—
    like enemies and Kosovo ripe for helping
     when occasion warrants beneficial
      injection of collateral, damage hard-sold
       and twitching so-soon to go out the door

sub-fragment (ii)

I
complicit
complicate
little Aussie Bleeders
black armband and court jester
booming out, like creole
in the breath and licking the lips
o how noble, oblige tainted or perfumed
in-circles. mission accomplished.

sub-fragment (iii)

Not exile—international
self-imposed citizen. Posted.

fragment 9
[halfway to the Hölderlin House]

You don't have to hold it all in
body or moment, not a container
    angry natures subdued

as the sun is closer
in particulars conditioned
as motorways pool and Byron
connects a generation
somewhere in or thereabouts
Greece always on his mind,
or near the tower, petri-dish stimulation
particular chemical responses
thanks to the woman at the health shop
who feeds the half-formed with salad—
an idea, half my social self
orbits alone bright in whose truth
brightens beyond belief
brightens with spring
as winter must come
spring summer and autumn
weighing less than it alone

fragment 10
[halfway, still]

but as I sit long
   on the river wall
      fighting an illogical sun—pleasure
       upsetting focal length
        dragged soothingly down

shattered glass circulates
   like a local flurry
      in steady mani-flow

each sliver a trace of Hölderlin
   dropped walking or a line lost
      by a visitor, wanting something

after purchasing a poem
　　each wraps in water; inner
　　and permanently spring—

at night, phosphor
　　diaspora, coming winter
　　nowhere is winter
　　　is or isn't

Epilogue
Hesperia—June—2020—1843—Ehrbarkeit—absence—
against the night sky—the burning village—

Sanctus, Sanctum: a love poem

i.

The smallest measure of matter
leaves traces before it vanishes:
the energy lost or exchanged
in cycling out to Grantchester
is love and prayer, duotone
landscapes and seasonal osmosis:
we were there, time wound back
like progress come unstuck,
the largest-ever hole in the ozone
layer, defined against the size of America.
A spoonbill larger than life,
mythological on its perch, dégagé—
as it should be, we'd guess.
That's back there, where we'd
be together if conditions were perfect.
Burnt white totem of the Avon Valley,
as if 'sedate order' watches over
communities and is positive
in a way we know it's not, like the Eloi
being everywhere in the English lyric,
or picnicking by an Australian river.
When the weather goes out of kilter
paragliders over Bakewell
drop as suddenly as they appear:
the spoonbill's beak's utility
becomes a rhythmic disaster:
isochronous: stress stress stress:
laneways where moisture clings
and growth meets rot and the cycle
plods its weary way. Holy, holy, holy.

ii.

That fox wrapped around
that roadsign—fashion piece
with flair, cured by the weather,
mummified. The Larrikin is in there.
Jokes about gender. Product
of nationalism, those soft endings,
para-rhymes and racism, bounties
and scalps and making a living.
Who cares? It's been up there
for weeks. People have seen it,
remarked on it: tasteless,
but then, they hold the hunt
for sheer pleasure and foxes
are despised: 'they eat the livers—
livers so small!—out of chickens,
and leave the rest'. Fox spot,
Kentucky Fried Fox, Red Fox,
why the hell not? The ads
fall apart, and that's what
selling's all about. There's no-one
to hear this as I mouth the words,
which reject the page,
the driving by, the twinkle
in the cavernous eyes
of a small head, teeth still shining,
needle-sharp.

iii.

A band strikes up a conversation,
and it's as if I'm there. Let's ditch
this stuff about centuries, about
Ages of . . . and grand alliances.

It's global chatter. I love,
I care . . . you know me.
And you know *this* doesn't
give life to THEE!
Poetry is a crematorium.
Love doesn't need it.
The Granta is thick with weed
and smart cars are bunched up
outside Lord Archer's house . . .
what more do we need?

Sine qua non

Those apples I've struggled to write
for years—lines about cooking
and fermentation and decoration:
haphazard globes denting as they crash
to the path, tepid in the first days
of autumn, enjambed like invocation—
of days apart, polished by humidity.
The collapsing moment: the thrill
of encounter, the sticky fluid
of memory spread like a blemish.
Those stray trees untended
glower like wild planetariums:
a pleasure I'd neglect, brought
so close to you, here in the past.

The Branches

Walking at night, blank stone
focussing streams of people, the branches
seem blacker than usual. Something
has happened, they mean to say,
residual warmth of late summer
dragging its heels through traces
of rain. The river, glassed over,
would deflect darkness,
were the crowds to notice.
So much iron; semi-ornate,
of an age when iron counted:
those almost too-sharp points
you wonder about falling on.
Cutting through to Storey's Way,
the infra-red a new superstition;
a call cuts a blank space,
a place where the blackest branches
drag sight, where song birds
were bright before dark,
when the owl was silent.

Field Notes from Mount Bakewell

for Harold Bloom

i.

Bark-stripped upper branches
of York gums—olive dugites
stretched taut, the dry blue
like stark black bitumen,
a torn limb from last night's
high winds, the snake struck
by a vehicle, maybe taking aim:
is it revenge when a snake,
tossed into the chassis, drops
and strikes the driver
searching for an oil leak?

ii.

The stubble a bed of nails,
or hypodermics mounted
on mixed-media, piercing
boot-soles, stapling socks—
soaked with blood that rubs.
Up there, through the burn-off
and parrot bush sown like mythology,
the harsh green of heat trees
mocks foliage—an idea
without history here,
on the hillside.
                    The launch-places
of paragliders—best thermals
for four hundred or a thousand
kilometres, depending on whom

you believe: where euros sweat
in small numbers and the minutiae
of reserves are transgressed
by stand of sheoaks: aerial mimics,
clarifiers of vegetable harmonics,
telecommunication dishes
microwaving panoramically,
ingesting and feeding
the collective soul.

iii.

Quartz outcrops packed in soil,
crumbling with sheep trails and frantic climbs,
sheoak, York gum, jam tree,
xanthorrhoea lean back to correct
the incline, against the vertical:
air comes out of the mountain
and fumes across the denuded spaces—
where drifts of pesticide settle,
brought by outside draughts.

iv.

'There is all day, all
day to go.'

                    Denise Riley

Locusts are starting to move
in small gusts, like plumes
or insistent waves
lapping at dry oats,
stubble. They rise up
like seed dispersal.

v.

In corridors and channels,
flurries, waves, and bands,
fed on first heat, undoing
in simultaneous languid
and accelerated sweeps,
NOT chaos, trite similes
don't work for them,
even Biblical comparisons
pall; like water spilt
over a hot surface?
Spitting dispersal?
Plague centre,
splitting to pass the mountain—
failing to reach the crown,
the trigonometrical station,
place of surveys
where altitude makes
for slight variations
in plantlife . . .
'Up top', tracks are cut
and bush is bashed,
yet locusts—so far—
are scarce. They happen
down there, like . . .

vi.

The last plague,
evoking red paint—delisting
gardens, chlorophyll
as blood and threatening
mad cow disease,
or its equivalent,

in locusts. Comparison
is often laconic.

vii.
Non-return valves
are standard in gardens
post- the drawback,
the payback from hoses
left in poison tanks,
sucked back, drawn back,
getting into the system.

viii.
Roos and bronzewing pigeons
can eat 1080 without suffering
ill effects? That they gut them
rapidly, to keep the eating
safe and sweet? The less said
the better.

ix.
Moving out towards Beverley:
a side journey past Mount Matilda.
Wagyl tracks: no growth,
shining like scales in the sun.
Below, the Avon snaking
its way towards the ocean,
siphoning or drawing
the flood. Swamp sheoaks,
flooded gums, the few deep
water holes remaining.
The rainbow begins or ends
on the Wagyl tracks, and there's

nothing romantic about it.
This is something else,
but the speaking won't fit
these lines: it has,
as do these lines,
its own precise science.
And the tides of the moon
rip through the undergrowth,
fire breaking the crusts of seeds,
the night shadows thrive
and growth is inflammatory.
On the day of a funeral
no stories are told
after dark . . . or six oclock,
depending on
the sun . . .

x.
Proximity unsettles chat,
the invitation: this body
wormed with holes,
locust-swarms
choking the labyrinth,
the owl bright on night's edge,
struck on rodents
electric, silently
and smokelessly firing
the vanishing grass.

xi.
The Amish sell corn
as Halloween approaches: a long way
from here, and a short time back.

American corn. Original,
or semi-original seed.
We make good
an exchange. Here,
at the base of the mountain,
a shearer grows corn.
He can plant and watch the growth,
despite injury. The pain
in his arm, in his head,
won't stop the silks forming.
Genetically engineered crops
are sweeping the district.
This corn grows steadily, daily.
The locusts have come. Let
them eat corn, he says, let them strip
the green before the seeds
have even come. They have
no choice, and I have no choice.
The insurance company
twists and turns, lies, hedges
its bets. Medical certificates
shoot the breeze. The locusts
tune in and out, changing frequencies.
No, they don't tell
the same story.

xii.
The road undoes the desire
to step generically: the locusts
so thick on their journeys
that snowfall or sandstorm
dictate coordinates. Like
diving and seeing sediment

flow past in the current,
as the day goes on
the flow increasing.
Like floaters in the eye
first distracting and
then forgotten.
Disaster brings
its minor reconciliations.
Judged monocultures,
comparatively speaking.

xiii.
Ground dyed blue by fallen
Paterson's Curse: in the cold,
brilliantly purple. Heat sheds and takes
their colour. Unlike the yellow
everlastings on the mount,
a different yellow,
as dry as paper,
but speaking out
against hungover skies:
clouds looming
in unsettled atmospheres,
the compass showing
its different faces.
Yellow flowers,
desiccating, to turn
suddenly transparent,
feeding back into the sun,
fuelling its reactions
and evocations.

xiv.

Bandwidth locusts mono rain
bending frequency interlock wandoo
rock sheoak the botanist
Ludwig Preiss, priority one taxon,
and, of course, *Thomasia montana*,
which I don't see: oedipal, unreceptive,
adjusting the bandwidth.

xv.

The guy from the chemical company
drinks a half-glass of Herbicide.
"There you go, harmless to humans."
The farmer, impressed, sprays
and gets his sheep straight back in there.

xvi.

                '. . . like fire and powder,
Which as they kiss, consume.'

Place of weeping, sleeping woman,
eloping against tradition
and cursed from bloodshed,
across the town,
across the region,
not hearing the warning,
the passion, the bleeding:
the mountains
breaking up and meeting,
reconciled as erosion
defeats them.

The Predominance of Red

Deployed against the snow,
A stark vocabulary,
Space between words and body,
An arrangement

As a perching bird
Might have it:
Deciduous narrative, tanagers
Busy at the feeders,

Or the crests of cardinals—
Quick impositions—
Caught picking at security—
Paranoid visions.

Can we declare witness
In the mirror-shattering
Inwardness
Of the pileated woodpeckers?

A nesting pair,
Declaring in winter—
Drumming up formulas,
Driving at the windows?

The heating system removes
Liquid from the air—a dry
Circulation, a redness
You can't declare.

And yet we're here,
Tapped co-ordinates
On a map bright and instant.
Ladder-backed woodpeckers

And tonal variations
Rioting the conscience;
As if we were always here,
As if local gestures

Were lost to the hum
Of blue light
That lies out there
Between

The dark and the weather,
Sun and red birds.

A Cardinal Influences Peripheral Sight

for Ron and Inese Sharp

Through insect screens
a patch of tangled
stems and leaves
works as graph paper;
or is this the way

it seems, in its duns
and browns? The snow-fray
an aura breaking up,
static scoriae . . .

We see community
and politics in the starlings'
feeding frenzy, hearted
deep by cardinal

working outwards,
its influence equally
peripheral through
the gridwork,

a blurring that bleeds
cross-species.
The failure of this
transcendent interlude

to contain colour
or snow glare
within the black reflector,
bares molten feathers,
blood vessels woven together.

Lyrical Unification in Gambier

for Marjorie

(i)

What remains barely the weather
report: sentencing labours of history
against all beginnings, the maples
leafless, the houses barely porous.

(ii)

I ride roads I am not familiar with,
a figure of speech, chrome strips
between windows. To the south,
burial mounds. Resolution
deep and simpatico. Northwards:
the lake effect, the snow plough.

(iii)

Deer go down to bow and gun,
roadkill is a 'cull': beauty
in the eye of rhetoric
keeps the engine
ticking over.

(iv)

Cornstalks like rotted Ceres'
thin black teeth. To end with this.
A season of political arrangements,
remnant snow quarried
like that pitiless ocean.

(v)
The driver must resist
all beauty, the smell
of an unfamiliar passenger.
A door rattles, the car
is almost new. It is shut
properly. Speed limit.
Farm machinery. A (solitary)
white field enclosed
by thawed pages.

(vi)
Maples, oak . . . all kinds.
A tornado ripped through here
three months ago and didn't
touch the houses either side.
Birds warble in the engine
cavity. A cord of wood
stretches out below
the kitchen window.
He says we listen
differently.

Diagnostics

Off-centre, the weaver finch
enjambs its neighbour, cluster
hedged deciduously against patina
and intensity. Briefly

it was blue as you
moved configuration
retrospectively, for now
it's a different truth;

gnosis epodes dogma
all agisting the form
and offerings: we eat
and give thanks and take

the flock low-to-ground
as granted. The depth of blue
only valid in red comparison,
these dulled birds gathered

collectively. We'd have
houses implosive,
as weather closes in
and snow turns to rain:

by this we recognise,
cross over, and make more
of time, as close to speech
as thought or garbled song.

Cultures

in memoriam Anna Rutherford

The islands are low to the water
and flat with heat—the birds
melt interiors, which spread
to the shore. There, the sands
shrink once more,
and contract to belief.

In other parts, the tune
of robins and finches
is small, and their red
tight as anxiety; inside
they outfly larger birds.

The texture of a feather
forms in language,
to the bird our first movements
vary, and expression
can be anywhere.

Rebellious, migratory
flights don't end up where
they're supposed to, and water
runs through the vista.
Sometimes we coincide,
now more than ever.

The Chambers: Prison Cells beneath the Nineteenth-Century Country Mansion, Western Australia

1.

In a darkness without chemi-luminescence
to challenge definition, no space
for comparison, tremors unsettled
the bricks, but not enough
to bring the walls down,
implode the chambers.

Beneath the house
with its antiques
and grand piano
ballroom opening out
like an invitation,
they enclosed.

Excavate, disinter, dig.
Exhume. Light fractures
and exchanges: heat, prayer.
So deep you wouldn't
have heard a sound up top
when prisoners devolved
into apparently random gradations
of pitch. The throat
a battered flute.

Unfamiliar birds
made as game birds,
field-fattened,

shrill in the ovens:
the black warrior's skin
stretched against the wall.
Body-heat tarnishing
architecture, the space
beneath, within.

2.

As a child led through narrowing passages
to the chamber with manacles and an altar,
that first sound of harpsichord,
Goldberg Variations. Down there,
a radio is static: nothing
comes in. Static is pater familias,
though the Church of England
sings here. A FLUX, luminary, organ glow, the form
                    of the body: the pain and grief
                    settled ritual prison life, a river beds
                    and flows nearby, the seepage
                    depths and whisperings
                    caught in bricks, sand, stone.

3.

Father gave his sons transistor radios
when they first hit the market:
they heard America,
and the cousins visited that house again.
You should go there. We should
do it together. You'd be scared.
Voiceover. Lies. Submission.

4.

The country kitchen opened out,
small abundant gods gesticulated
from hot places, from the cool
of the cupboards. Heavy stone
and high roofs kept the driving summers
out: a stranger performed tricks
with fruit over the wooden floorboards.
He sang ballads. He dressed up—
sharp shoes, red dress, rouge—
and recited 'The Man from Snowy River'.

5.

Water damage. Speak trenched spirit,
impudent light of depth, pressure, crush.
Sheep nudging at the garden.
An imported palm sways in the searing wind.
Speech in the morning. Evening sense
loses fathoms. We asked you here
to state your case: location,
co-ordinates. Movements
of the peoples.

6.

Accused, fruit falls
from the place of the eyes.
Lightning lit hilltops
and fire raced down. Below ground it was cool,
though they sweated. The house went up quickly.
Labyrinths of title deeds and planning permissions,
inheritance, death tax, changes in governments:
a compact whirlwind cut the garden,

cutting dates out of papers.
In the static it seeped in,
we know that all this is proof.
Proof: this theory, this transubstantiation:
the bells as confident as stone,
proof heard, turned to story.

House Eclogue

Host
This wooden frame might be your own
pinned with steel at the joints, riven
to foundations set in friable earth;
seat of the gentry in the country
where masques are performed
like DNA, perfectly cloned
in this rural setting, seeded
just after sunrise, deep
in the woods. Don't let it
alarm you, the blood-bird's
black face, the heart-pickings
as stale as its migratory flight.
Welcome, eat and drink
as you see fit. What is ours
is yours—the household gods
are gregarious and hungry,
and glow with confidence.

Guest
Typically kind of you, a reputation
confirmed in the city. I apologise
for bringing sickness between these walls,
violating this taboo. Censer
skies swing low and yet light
fills every space, language is crisp
and alive and values lost outside
thrive. These photos of your family,
the soiled shoes by the doorway,
polished floorboards and mandala rugs,

reproductions of Vermeer and Homer,
speak of quiddity and agency.
The potatoes turn green quickly, I hear?

Host
We have a kitchen full of refreshing herbs,
of oils and brews to drive your sickness out:
we'll restore you with supplements.
Our grandfather built this house,
and called it ecumenical. Blessed
by every guest who has set foot in it.
It is like an organism living in symbiosis
with its occupants—guest-hosts
all of us, in this place where
flora and fauna grow against
adversity, illuminate the cavities.

Guest
Sealed in against the cold the sick air
will circulate, warmed to blood-heat,
pumped and piped. Plasterwork
inscribes the wallflesh, basement
and attics role-play extremities.
In that room she prays,
in there they're having sex.
Good or bad karma, a history.
In the century-old baby photograph
old men look grim on three-month-old bodies.
There is cable and a decent stereo.

Host
The piano harmonises perfectly
with the stereo. In the basement

they dressed the kill. Bone, skin,
fur—wool carpet. Extractions
and sealants. Chairs for carving.
A kitchen vegetable garden.
The lawns neatly cut: gathering,
focussing. The porch seat.
The lost toy in the sandiest place.
Please sign the guest book.

Guest
Colours embalm in the darkened room
as if love is loud and hate desperate;
critical of mountainous blankets,
rivers in the sheets. Dead skin
and the signature of fluids
are loud on the floor. Light doesn't
always show dialogues. I narrate
like a spy indoors, to undo reputations,
immaculate as a character reference.

Poltergeist House Eclogue

Woman
You wait until we're alone in the house;
unsettling, destabilising, contra-indicating,
as if all should be calm here, not said
nor implied, the hum of the heating,
thermostat quavering, as if to prelude,
forewarn, distort a family photo.
This relationship is threadbare,
hanging on by a thread at best.

Poltergeist
Upset is not random, carefully planned
strategy, tactics are honed.
Council, community, mutual
understanding. Between us, a pact.
I move, we move, they move, only
where you want us to. Expectation,
tenterhooks, the book crashes to the floor—
you're on the other side of the table.
A seismograph registers, recording
at interstices of the body.

Woman
Investigate, don't run at first
provocation, imagine chance and external
occurrences, imagine distress
coming to a head: time-loss, faith
diminishing. A bird flew into the house
and dashed itself against the windows.
The light sharp outside, though frost
on the ground. I let it out. And still
books fell. And fall. We listen.

Poltergeist
Energy is data, first lesson we learn.
It has its own propaganda. Sexfeed,
screaming matches, making up . . .
things not bargained for. It's like
a package holiday. Like a shift
in the television schedule: she
searches hard beyond the image,
in there, amongst circuitry.

Woman
Small things falling, moving, almost
acceptable. But faucets all on or the carpets
changing colour anger me.
The threat of exorcism is tense in the house.
The worse it gets the less I mention
these goings-on. Just store it up,
verging on critical. The radio comes on.

Poltergeist
Leaving a situation is both hard
and comforting. You know someone
as much as you ever will if it's
that far gone. And you can't take
them with you, you go out alone.
As scripts and formula are written
and spoken, I turn the wine to water.
I send cracks through plaster.
I turn stomachs. We are gone.

The Gift

for Mirjana Kalezic

Snow so fine trees titanium white,
their black veneered, crows charged,
jagged choristers loudly bright
as residue sharpens outlines;

prayer suffers
no loss in translation
and scripts village air
as it might an aria—the bird

blackens to glean the city,
the temples open outwards.
A word migrates and sublimates
snow's hydraulics

and what we take from tableaux
infringes balance;
stark silence indemnifies
the lightest of birds

articulate beyond our windows,
so fast they still the eye,
imply a familiar scene,
tangential flight-paths.

First Essay on Linguistic Disobedience

The less I see the bird
the more the bird is there, a bird less seen? I follow
it chit chit chit, verbally
awkward, passive in its small communities.
Red as always. This lyrical certainty, a linearity as
    'comforting' as
Leaves of Grass.
The same sport of democracy
offsetting the house,
the open garden,
the field others wander through.
They designed it themselves.

Joggers surround the house
and ice drops sharp.
There are no curtains
and the joggers look inwards—
machines, made on government treadmills.
The less of, the more: better kinder
that way. Better
words wanted in better orders:
not the syntax? Note: the tribes driven inwards
as if Ohio might be a name-home, or preconnecting
burial mounds, death-homes, enclosures.
Crypted over, the house plans
fill room on room, the electrical wirings,
the colour-coded circuits.

In the valley the fraternity
has left refuse and a dead turtle: cans and black stockings—
    nylons—

adorn the targeted tree. Deer move swiftly by, white high-tailing it
out of there. Security assure
it's not black magic, and that there
are no shell casings.
In the early morning skunks are shot
by skunk hunters: skunks root the ground over,
searching for grubs. A repellent chemical
is sprayed on golf courses—
where it doesn't reach, the skunks
de-green the surfaces.

These anxieties strut about the houses,
species outside a bird book.
What's wrong out of this talk,
these whispers behind closed doors?
Justly, this is our prison.
I entreat the gardener and itinerant labourer,
the seed-drill and combine harvester,
or the snake brought in with the firewood,
deep sleep as just as the governing
instinct. Protect the snake. Trusts us?
The strength is in its poison
and the power of its jaws to deliver.
The body-spring.

I give this language nothing
the birds' sing-song translates as a forest
denuded of trees: these wooden houses
working for nothing.
As if the progress of seasons
doesn't add up—
alienated by smog and effluent,
blue tarpaulins flapping in the wood,

rites of initiation.
The grandfather—mine—was of some
Masonic order and I knew nothing
of it. Parrots are red birds
where I come from, home-
shifting, testing density
of surfaces. Beneath, communities.
The pipes rising up, copper-clouded water
pooling where the parrots' taxes
run out.

Second Essay on Linguistic Disobedience: the masculine houses of America and wavering Australian echoes . . .

'But it is easier to deal with the real possessor of a thing than with the temporary guardian of it.'

—Thoreau

'The room in which I found myself was very large and lofty.'

—Poe

'When we moved into this new residence, we formally christened the place "Waldmere,"—literally, but not so euphoniously, "Waldammeer," "Woods-by-the-Sea,"—for I preferred to give this native child of my own conception an American name of my own creation.'

—P. T. Barnum

Lorca and Baudrillard, protagonists, real possessors, looking
    for refreshment,
though speech is the only old-growth forest left standing,
all forests are data and material for houses,
all signs in LANGUAGE; courtesy
has us polite in the houses of friends and strangers,
at home we'd be vocal, possibly loud! bone and ligament
coerce vistas, LANDSAT caught in the canopy,
the interiority of the surfaces of the crown
of the Chrysler Building, and oh Liberty, green in the waters
    of empire,
the lookouts of Diamond or Gloucester Tree,
the thin slices and patches of old-growth karri
near Pemberton and the blackmail of tourism;
the fog over the Stirling Ranges gives the impression
if memory serves us correctly

of being the same fog suffusing the woods at the end of North
   Ackland Street,
Gambier, or flying over the crags of the Rockies; before the advent of
   the street
there was no wood, just forest; skunks turned the earth over
and groundhogs swelled in their burrows,
there were variegated red birds, but rhetorical red
wasn't dominant, not in the same way, not in the way of blood from
   jam trees
or the core-wrench of rosellas; the tamma lives in the region of the
   town of Tammin,
a wheatbelt town, famed for accommodating the initial
grain silo shaped out of concrete—geowise, this is a long way from
Mount Toolbrunup in the Stirlings that offers little shelter though
   just down the road
where rare karri stands in the Porongurups might devolve into
   materials
and guns in the forest, this idea of machine, machine-driven idea
is expedient in the vast distance between the New World 'down
   there', and the older New
World here, this America, this inspirer of blue books scripted in neon
and highly refined ink, deciduous and Episcopalian, restless cradle
   of synagogue
and mosque, refugees from Tibet, 'wetbacks' from across the border,
Spanish eating English with English being made simpler to prevent
   this happening,
virtue to sustain the breakup of Microsoft, or copyright and Napster
and artistic integrity that's profit, the soul's growth
polite and well-mannered and stamped onto the barrel
of a Desert Eagle magnum, ownership a collective
grammar; Pine Gap and Exmouth, AWACS curving the horizon,
like the mother waiting on the shore in Horace, waiting for her son
to return, comforts below ground, the consumer screen

and parasitic non-denominational
'placid pastoral' Australian Government,
busy with the nail gun and hardwood from Borneo;
as if to set up the nurturing, the clone-factories, the tyranny of the
    XY chromosome,
even when the committee is run by women, the foundation stones
    laid down
by a team with a girl apprentice, taking shit from the blokes
and putting up with it, the laws holding back rivers of severed timber
trucked from private property: transgress immediately? The tamma
is a marsupial, a small marsupial, agented by injustice,
disgraced by association of name and place, the courtesy
of settlers and neighbours as government, as eradication or neglect
    or the planks taken
from the sea of the forest must be restored though our houses fall
    and are no longer built,
and even the low scrub is gone as a windbreak,
this sick patriotism to vernacular as homogeny is just a new hege-
    mony,
the body parts of the echidna intertwined with a skunk's architraves,
pitch not quite perfect, though transgenic as highways and wild pigs
demolished in forests as sport: trans is desire,
leaf-litter on the floor, turning to humus,
polishing the boards.

Third Essay on Linguistic Disobedience

for Ron

'We can, at any time, double the true beauty of an actual landscape by half closing our eyes as we look at it.'

—Poe

'(Where "flaw," signifying a sudden gust or spell of stormy weather, is indeed fine.)'

—Steiner

'all these phenomena are important'
—Moore

Distance brings thoughts of the driveway at York,
red clay bled up through the gravel overlay,
blood of jam tree pooling on its edges. Property: a taxonomy
of stills and rushes, trials and legacies, gift-gifts
and a banded snake coiled in the house, in a cupboard,
or a gwarder flexing intuition under the door.
After a sudden and rapid decline, my eyesight steadied—over
the years, three increments along these lines. New locations
brought redecoration, scenery coming in patches, in fragments,
wrought like paper fibres. Physical conditions altered,
and some days were grainy, but the senses found a system.
The venom of snakes built up over these long winters.
In coastal areas the yellow-bellied sea-snake
floundered out of water, or oared its way
skilfully past near reef-breaks. The skill
is the subject. Leaving, this is what's remembered.
Filling out the picture, Mount Brown glowers as light collapses;
backed by a fair approximation of certainty,
Mount Bakewell circumflexes, fuses synapses.
The snakes here are apparently abundant though harmless,
and we'll walk in the long grass,

fearless. A small revolution, he went out
without rechecking and rechecking the lights, the stove, the faucets;
the value of this is not equitable in currency terms;
as a thing to barter, it has special worth. The hand pump
in the field is a rusty icon without utility,
and it is fine to have stormy weather engage
with it, albeit too frequently. That tree down
is a sign of things out-of-hand, and we spend ourselves
retelling it. Having only half-opened her eyes
she was pleasantly surprised to see more by opening them.
Sharp lines delineated, and the maple insisted.
Authority was challenged, as if it was important.
Trust that flaws are fine, that landscapes
are always half present: apportioning crow noise
to one part of the house leaves us bereft,
that's the counterfeit: tribute is not restitution,
I feel obliged to walk to the fringe of property
and look out, infuse the pink-and-greys flocking in with neap tide
of heat and humidity, the movement
vaguely sexual, but displaced at moments.
A triple-spiked seed, as hard as granite,
from elsewhere: caltrop, cal trope calt rop
picked up on soles and creeping over red dirt,
an emblem, motif, coat-of-arms,
the paper is vocal, a program of spray and dissembling
burns like static in the conducive air.
The pair of black-shouldered kites has gone elsewhere
and yet still I'd make you welcome,
apportion time, plant grevilleas
to hedge against erosion, as flawed
we fly the coop, the bungarra
tongue-lashing at our doorstep.

Fourth Essay on Linguistic Disobedience

'A text is not a text unless it hides from the first comer, from the first glance, the laws of its composition and the rules of its game.'

—Derrida

'Know all men by these presents, that I, Henry Thoreau, do not wish to be regarded as a member of any society which I have not joined.'

—Thoreau

Taking the fifth, he avoided the traffic. The organism
wasn't feeling comfortable, though the sun bright and everything
   blue.
In the canyons, prayers are trapped halfway; cooling,
eventually dropping—churned up by pedestrians and cars. Advocacy
redecorates, brings in old fireplaces, pronounces
death-again sentences on leather chairs.
I have no clubs and no belonging, though the marks—amatory,
   elegiac, territorial,
arbitrary—left by beak of ladder-backed woodpecker, or the claws
of the twenty-eight parrot, on the bark of differing geographies,
erase none of my loyalties. This is not romanticism.
Continuation of lines of branches and twigs in the leafless woods
takes us back, imploded to fractals, hesitant at the solid point
of interruption: soundless. In the rock-garden
skinks move out of the tepid, a willy-willy
weaves garlands out of the crop: gamenya,
tall and high on protein. This house is stranded in that field,
the roof is giving way and red brick crumbling.
There's a well nearby fed by a spring. Salt-rings
mark decline. Birds here are shunned
and strings of fragments come undone.
What's of me here? he asks, memory
faster than time, the whole lot imploding.

His auntie will not visit the farmhouse she raised
children in; her new place is decorated with photos
of the old place, a curatorial space. Recently he went out
to take a look, preparing a report then abandoning it to a carmine
     sunset—
insects thick on the windscreen. The twenty-eights tracked the car
as always, white cockatoos abandoned mallee trees.
At the cross-roads a shearer or young driver
cut sick: figure-eights and 'doughnuts' engraved deep.
On the sign at the corner of Mackey and Cold Harbour Roads,
a fox was impaled—its tail bristled like headgear.
Bounty hunters call it 'poling', or 'shishkebabing'.
It's what you do with 'foreign muck'. A sharp taste
in their food brings it on. The Needlings burnt without
touching the paddocks—it doesn't happen like this anywhere else,
as far as we know. Sheep spread out evenly,
as if placed to make something happen.
Belonging to this is not desirable.
Unbelonging, I make conversation
with like-minded people. A wedge-tailed eagle is seen
on a fence-post and none of the party wants to shoot it. I select
this society. The guns will overwhelm you! a sceptic declares, safe
in the anonymity of the world wide web. We will absorb
consequences. Sun burns even in winter here,
skin mutating. Its despotic face is passionate and unrelenting,
making language form. A spoonbill sifts units of water,
silt-heavy and charged with mosquito larvae,
in the gulch, creek, ravine, stream, gulley . . .
solubility, intactness . . . not a technical piece in a legal sense,
an 'impressionistic' account as a means of redress,
just ice concurrent with heat.

Fifth Essay on Linguistic Disobedience
in memoriam A. R. Ammons

'that I could live lively as you
 and have
 no more to die . . .'
                    Ammons

Memorandum: 'The soul is a region without definite boundaries.'
A heat wave and a blizzard,
and mud cones, swollen, hanging heavy
on the leafless branches of maple trees:
through other geographies,
we'd guess wasps or gall insects,
though it could be something
outside this logic; it's what's given up—
certainty, the positive side of taking
for granted; wind-whip and clarity
cross-cut white, what's dormant
or unseen in effect, concurrent.
Inland tidals machine friction and lake effect,
tail-ended down here, edibly durable,
within storehouses of movement: deer lists,
familiarity hosting property sanctuary and wind-chill factors
tripping scales, sealed in by snow, reading Borges,
so stilled and turned inside out, fractures
bound together upland, downtown, clustered.
The plants have grown apart, and exposed in space
historicity pumps them up—locale, region, neighbourhood.
By these directions, you'll find them relative
to viewpoints handed-down or retold out
of convenience: the bitumen road narrows and turns to gravel

and a sentinel horse—'the statue'—stands blinkered
on the corner property, 'they' don't seem to care.
Then at the cross-roads, turn left and then the next left
and then the second right, bitumen
gives way to gravel. Pleasure
is nowhere to be found,
unless the brown hawk, preyless,
and watching for rodents,
is confident. We can't know that,
heightened at dusk, bats radically sounding,
the hill backdrop eating perspective,
what haven't we sanctioned?
What haven't we heard
between crows unsettling
on lower branches, draining darkness,
the night brighter than before?

.

Sixth Essay on Linguistic Disobedience: 100 days after the inauguration of the men who advise Bush

'Threshold gifts mark the time of, or act as the actual agents of, individual transformation.'

—Hyde

'Writing is neither remembering nor forgetting neither beginning or ending.'

—Stein

'. . . one's intellectual vision is not a disembodied mental activity; rather, it is closely connected to one's place of enunciation, that is, where one is actually speaking from.'

—Braidotti

'Even earlier than Egyptian timber-house coffins, hut urns appear in the fertile crescent. The notion of cremating the dead and burying their remains in a model of a house is as diffused as the cremation rite itself.'

—Lotus 8

'This is not Democracy—it is savagery. It shows the glutton hunt for the Dollar with no thought for aught else under the sun or over the earth.'

—Sullivan

Melt is variable, tacks grass tufts and declines,
gradates around creeks, seasonal irregulars,
expected in time; that glare dishevelled,
insists. Here, speak. Between pictograms,
woods increase, believed as we'd be, those terminal
repletions. At this point the house offered
recesses and terraces, castings from old diggings
freedoms and structure, dwelling: abide honour,

this riparian coming to share, for here's
hidden almshouse, onlyhouse, versehouse,
singing windows, breakout, grating
fenestration, iron and metal, semiflow.
They bring leaving and crossing, bird-types
shape and colour, repetitious patterns
of tree and wall poems. Speech text
written, scorch-drift clearly white,
and this other lighting; scarce topography
not looking, minding pleasure
and the cuckoo—I notice weaver finches,
striations in bare bushes, uneasy over their dead,
mouthing food. At the highpoint, the wooden
firewatch tower. A grandfather. A family
naming. From there his men looked out,
over. Charred at the base, unstable,
fire encircled. A house stilt-walking
but stuck. That's the grandchild. Four, maybe five.
He remembers large batteries with brass terminals.
For the telephone: the wire out of there.
Jarrah, blackbutt, cuts filled with young pines.
Sound isolation: trunk chimneys, walls of scrub,
vault bruised yellow, grey, black . . . ectopic reds.
Correspondence lessons—even—closed
indefinitely. Math suffered: trees burnt
beyond counting. Volatility sine curve,
sin curvature, though pluming out.
The pall segue, heat exchange, capillarity:
in the spacious New York apartment near Union Square
an animal is carved and leather works as adjective.
Birds, strung to walls, like books.
Muscular taut language smelling only faintly musty.
Woman draped arctic fox over a well-tooled

leather coat sexualised in the library.
No care taken for flaws, the president
considers it good advice. Inscribed tree rings, dark tailings,
pharmakon faith-based registers up-hill: treasury,
temple to Apollo, stadium. Monti di pietà/
damna et interesse; fauces, atrium, tablinum,
ale, portico, hoisting machines. Brother governor
says we'll win in Florida. Psychic written death-taxed
penalty acting out buzzard memorabilia,
buckshot rains down there, centrally appointed.
Cadre, declension in the House's
black mirror, nightmare mechanics, dimensional
chat via pastoral motif, mannerisms
spiritually illumined.

Seventh Essay on Linguistic Disobedience: Rejection of Landscape through Body-Map

'This, then, is what I want to address. First, how are the angels
present in nature, and second, what does the act of imitating the
action of angels entail?'
—Sardello

Punctured sole-skin, game of Twister
farmers said would end up with blacks
winning out, poor white kid a tangled mess,
landless, language all hit-n-miss, as if . . .
decorative, script succoured soft cliffs,
eroded, wind swept down and out,
Red Cross passports and nationless
creativity ex nihilo, void like self
on thresholds of disconcerting tortured animals
joke equinox, utterance, like lists,
like forsythia and four snows ensuing,
like Ensign Dale transporting Yagan's head to Britain;
see this edge, as we hate and conceal
and scarify, tch tch, as counter-compromised,
hawks not there for you, this walk, these steps
highlighting sycamores and conifers, let's delete
the contrast: Amish buggy, black as global networking vans,
as vistas are unlayered, we collect plastic containers,
effete, winged, farmtools at public auctions,
see THIS threshold, this clysmic recondition,
blackening rendition as another matter
drives and eats us out—you see we,
stringing angels in genetic trees,
as Arabic in fifteenth-century Africa
transliterates speech,

written as, undoing body text
and words in the canopy, ringing
changes, connecting families,
valuing no two cultures, no truth or beauty
binaries, etymologies regardless,
synched as packaged, for that's Kulture!
Give us multi, from standing room only
to rarefied spaces, servitude and swans' heads
under white cloths: there's your proof,
you are what you question-mark,
like a signature, gentleman scholar.
In four days green consumed and scaped,
seed-proof, evidence; unbodied,
scatter erotics and wrath,
prime matter close to the heart:
cardinals and parrots
totem-shifting datelines
speech remnants,
revelation's backburners,
a murder of crows.

The Shed

Comes before the house—domicile
on the cleared block. Prelude
to building permission. The Shire
never quite turns a blind eye,
but you can sweat it out in summer
and shiver in your sleeping bag
in winter, the reinforced concrete
floor a proverbial slab of ice.
The jerry-built living quarters
grow quickly dark with cooking
and food residue, despite clean habits.
At night, the grinder throws plumes
of sparks up into grey air.
Lighting is never adequate.
The breakdown of stainless steel
on emery paper is dramatic,
and the intensity of the sound
is its own simile. It would be
an unhealthy jet engine it was compared
to: ignition, eruption, exhaustion,
to the power of ten. The sparks
don't make up for the lack of light.
They suck light from the darkest places
and exhaust it: sucked dry, burnt out!
Outside, the tawny frogmouth scans
for rodent heat and movement, which
is also a play with light. Clarity
has a different meaning here—out of the shed
it might be best to use another
vocabulary. Small stands of jam tree,
redgum, the odd spotted gum,

have been left with the clearing;
internationalists would prefer
their presence wasn't referred to,
though they might enjoy the shade they cast
in summer. But the dweller of the shed
wants only to know this location.
You wouldn't call him a regionalist;
he thinks about gender. Half-light
solidifies the spaces between letters.
Language is a long solid run, continually
wrapping itself round. The potbelly
stove expands illegally, its light the glow
of combustion. Smoke collects moisture
and falls to the gulley, where foxes
move carefully—he would never say
they lurked—unable to settle confidently
to building the next stage of their occupation.
In the scrap lumber piled next to the shed
wall, mice move freely. The tawny frogmouth
is probably aware of their presence,
and might be waiting—the sound of the grinder
diminished, then gone. Conjunctions
lost, night-talk enjambed
in the trusses overhead, panels
of corrugated iron rippling with the lifting
wind. Bike frames, motors from washing machines,
peanut paste jars filled with nails and washers,
fireplaces and doors from demolished
Federation houses, three-legged wicker chairs
unwinding like family stories, odd shaped
panels of metal whose history is lost,
encoded nowhere, a sack of offcuts
from black sheep, a cement-mixer powered

by a motor from somewhere else. These
are mapped in halfsleep, only seen
before work, or on days off.
Soon, very soon, the house
will be built.

Through Vertical Blinds

The widow presupposes faux brick
and a steady run of suitors, pre-war
colonial, with manners and operatic
gestures potentially in place:
it was pounds not kilos, 'imperial'
and not Bonaparte's march across Europe,
which in the lingo was tyranny,
the shipping containers they store
prisoners in at Canning Vale, an hour
or two's drive south of here—time being
that non-specific—like convict brigs.
In the early winter sunlight
the mountain schisms along perforated
folds of a geological timeline,
radio loud at the place downroad,
back-hoes and oxy-acetylene
augmenting bright bird processes.
The work of the place is filters,
suspect politics keeping the coarse grains
from the finer compounds, through clean sand
it almost gets molecular, and in oil filters
is chemical. You were at primary school
when they converted from inches to centimetres,
when you suddenly seemed much taller.
Your self-image temporarily prospered.
In the seed bins you shovelled towards
the eye of the funnel, an almost precise
point, but just vague enough to alter
certainties of the body, with formative
suspicions—but then that rusty nail
really did bring on a tetanus shot, and cows

were slaughtered out of this certainty.
The bright and dull sides of vertical
blinds suggest an equation—a glider
on the field of vision, interdiction.
But this is primarily sheep country
and they hope for better markets—
rescue-animals secure
on the small property.

The Trial

Imposing sharecropper or woodcuts
As reportage, expressionist interiors,
Away from the coast, the spread of rainfall
A test: the short intense growing season,

The rapids drying off—hard-headed,
Banned strains modulating, the contracted
Pollination, surveillance, and classification;
Disbanded outside the undeclared spectacle,

The box or ringside seats only. Power
Fibrillates along the ridges: bubbles of mist
And trepidated outline that might mass
In the city: reproductions, gifs, jpegs,

Downloadable at all times, docile and strangely
Disciplined. The masonry wasps build mud chambers
On *Fifteen German Poets*, locked in a shed,
Hearing the voices of disorder and compaction.

Escaped from their trial plots, the NEW lupins
Form movements, compatible only with NEW lupins,
Partitioning traditional lupins, the few 'natives'
Left to the edges. There will be detente

The company assures us, like a card trick.
A stark simile that aches to be obvious.
The hollow stems of lupins split and snap.
Flock birds name, un-name, and rename selves.

'We didn't really know what they were up to . . . given
They trial all sorts of things in there . . .';
It's a valley here, and chainsaws rip semi-dead
Wood for cast-iron hotboxes—the cold is its own.

Thick smoke and creosote, but rich ash
For the garden. This, the 'analytical space',
Documentary, those 'fractions of reality',
A family went in and named the river.

The Semiotics of a Truck Overturned in Fog

As if it just slipped from under me,
this umpteen-wheeler, this slice of America,
made by a company that converted army trucks,
made them bigger and better, hauling logs
out of the dark heart, fuelling the rush
for expansion and comfort; this industry
I pilot, over canals and rivers of tar, far out
through the crops and grazing spaces,
cleared places that grow yellower
with each kilometre, even in winter.
This early morning sun molten in fog,
diffuse like beer, the barrels rolling
down the hill, thudding then muffled
as if the metal's turned liquid, something grinding,
maybe the engine sickly ticking over,
and somewhere sheep and parrots.
Through fog I see a red haze pulsing
on a periphery, the vast bulk of the truck
looming up out of its cracked spine, angles
ridiculous, this leviathan, this lifeblood
to distant places, who'll know me
as their pubs run dry, who'll curse me
as the fog lifts and cranes elevate
my broken livelihood, front-end loaders
shovelling kegs onto trailers attached
to other contractors' vehicles,
and strangers stretchering me
into a day that will be supremely bright,
once the fog has lifted.

On the Rejection of the Term "Property" for This Place

Locating the ensign normative on the questboat
of inner mappings, survey betoken, the flock
beknights the leader; split lupins, so enriched
they triple protein, as upwind predators
gurgle in their juices. Situate the predicate,
distil sand filters, oil patches where sumps
have dumped their turgid loads, where it's
not quite happy for journalists—that's where
they made the Aborigines. Corrugations, Boolean,
iron and galvanising, bedevilled in sutures
as down cycle, or business in speech, as if licences
or feathers, good eating a deployable, a summons
or magnetic. Corporate, modelled in the model of,
modality and detainees, to keep the envelope
pure; all waves confer against the next
though come in sets, and the king wave lifting
out of nowhere, by far the biggest. It links
coastals and whale soundings with fingers and combs
of John Deere platforms. No respect, they enslave
as collective—single mass of categories,
whipper snippers on Council edges, cutting down
to median strips, testing radars just outside
the station, the 40k in-town limit. This property,
permissions legal and moral, siphoning petrol
on pre-unleaded cars, stopcocks in sheep
watering troughs, the length of barbed wire
and odd echidna on the fringe of language.
The French were almost here, in force; primo-
geniture, this periodic tabulation of rare earths
and growth rates, the university letting infantile

eureka and big buck visions through considerable
holes in the wire, like old crank telephones
and local exchange. Barrier comedown on the home
trading range, with confidence, with bluster,
this corner of property, 1861, good stone
despite the trouble: family: Cornwall,
Scotland, Ireland, London. The city as country,
siting ownership as event horizon, trial and consequence
the mesh and tribute; kin and cure, constructing
social ills, devouring science fiction nervous
in the ancient outhouse. They wipe on newspaper.
The print pollutes the fissures. A Nyoongah friend
says they speak within the family, and family
is always someone else's, as well as memory.
Personal and shared, this continual habitation, Hansard
and despair. Lipservice counts like letters to the paper,
with their colour photos of teenage prostitutes.
Readers await the coming of the demagogue,
the harbinger of prejudice. Damn her! And damn
archaeology and anthropology and the oily wash
from the Avon River; slip clutch, vee belt, running
rough as guts, as long as it takes to cross the crop
stepping gingerly, or ripping-it-up in the ute,
flat-tack bashing the shit out of the shockies,
always a target. We have permission to cross,
multiple orders, letters of approval, up to the mountain,
footheld on ridges, marking time the native grasses.
Scientific name . . . approbation of guilt, or to collect
chunks of childhood preserved as faded everlastings,
protected now. Clods of clay, resinous soil,
currents freed up in the rock-picked basin,
pools of sediment, and wells as eyelets
like old campfires ringed with conversation,

as if it could all be reconstituted. Here, sanctuary
is a division within division, say quarter or half
a hectare, even an acre. Rarely on the roadside
the dead kangaroo, that twenty years ago
made roo bar 'essential' equipment.
At the gateway, rabbits dig into soft banks,
just beginnings. Down past rail lines
lights even-out across town, streetlights intense, macro-
engagements with darkness—for the protection
of citizens and properties. Courthouse.
Flyscreens. Early photographs. Dartboards.
The various dreams to be had at intervals
through seasonal labours, muddy boots, socks
and shirts shot with haycarting, that slick of residue
from all applications deemed necessary—pastoral
paranoia barely wreaks havoc in the working
habits of the city, or the foothills. Number plates.
In the breakup, the centre piece went to the least
land-hungry, who sold it at a profit to the most
land-hungry, so they'll not be getting it back
if fortunes improve. Centrifugal, topsoil
climbing up fence-posts, last of the hardwood,
genetic material barely stable, uprights in the crown,
as families lose touch during periods of intensive
sunspot activity. Caught between obligations
and permissions, bands become belts inside the body,
rusty engine cavity. Provenance. Tenure. Landfill.

The Crest

That at high speed this rise
moving away from town can so much
epitomise the age; the limit
reached just before the crest,
narrowing down to a bottleneck,
a noose of gravel shouldering
the long thin black neck, and then
the truck, prime-mover
full to the gunwales with tractor
parts, as heavy as you'd like
on asphalt contracting after
an intense summer, this crest,
slipshod movement, fatigue or surprise
or early morning sun in the eyes,
undoer of families and georgic
sentiments, vacuum flask forcing
together iconic auto-manufacturers
of different continents, as nearby
a twenty-eight wanders about the crushed
body of another twenty-eight, you'd guess
a partner, so early in the morning, in the cold
the fog not long lifted, the coffee
from the roadhouse warm and hyping-
up the flesh. And she thinks: I wonder
how he's going getting the kids
ready for school, as the truck
approaches town, crest, apex,
the becoming-one: crosses on a roadside.

Hay Bale Collected Off Road

It's the roads we blame for progress,
a word already anachronistic—just not
quick enough! Long tidings, criss-crossed
roundabout, ringed stretches of connections,
all points between points, straight and curving,
dishevelled but gleaming. Pot-holed, we racket
along, teeth chattering, bones squeaking,
verbs and adjectives conflating. Hallelujah!
Famine roads, late input of convict labour here—
this State sought it out and clung for dear life.
Compressors and rollers, blokes in panel vans
with radioactive stickers—it's all in the density—
unpack the Bomb. Cold-shouldered, the littered
highway, national clean-up days linking
the entire country; migrant communities
might venture out—they say non-Europeans
had better sit close to the speed limit
and keep on going. The roads here pass through.
Widening gravel tracks into gravel roads,
firewood collects, the gravel-throated yawp
of bulldozed wandoos, the petrified networkings
of other species. Who and what travels through
the rural watch. Tyre brands intensify, hiss
and stick, fast-track rip-off adhesive strips,
or sharp cut of blade on ice, as flat-strap
the slippery slide to milepost, reflectors
prophetic and cabalisitic. Some rumours
get through, but not as many as traffic
might indicate. Counters, tonnage, cops
with scales weighing up favours and privileges;
firm but of an ilk, barely ecumenical.

And then rounding the slow-down to ninety
ks in the road, a hay bale, still bound
but pushing fragmentation, yellow brick of tufts,
an accident waiting to happen. Almost skidding to a halt,
off-centre, hoiked into the boot. Think of the sheep!
And then a few minutes on, the lumbering truck,
bales neatly stacked—somehow the stray bale
doesn't add up, mathematically anywhere
on the land would be imprecise. The parish
has reached its limits, the congregation
perfectly balanced—tenor and mezzo-soprano—
allotment of children, women who still
sell cakes, blokes who'll hop in and put up
a kit home in a weekend. So, overtaking,
the hay remains silent if not subdued
in the boot, hunched driver
of the hay truck barely suspecting.
Shot way on, an overtaking lane—
could have waited, but just wanted
to get on with it, enjoying the rush.

Lighting the Bushman Fire Before the Others Rise

Sun crisp on the curve of Bakewell
is lymphatic in the gulley—coldest point
fused with flock of pink-and-grey galahs
scattering enigmatically; sear flux
in confused canopy, what is light,
flesh, feathers? I step out for kindling
and cut wood, the air grating
neck and shoulders ache, like sand
in the works. A nervous remnant
of last evening's feud works its tic:
the horse woman of the hill
and her dozen horses of the apocalypse
riled . . . then stilled: the tension
permanent? Galahs razz and shriek,
layering chronology. The door
nudged open, and the wood deposited
at the foot of the Bushman stove. Iron box.
Window to conflagration.
Everything here is Biblical—you don't
choose to write it. Opening the door
to history, the pattern of setting.
In the burning there will be no rights.
Under the wood bark: insects,
minute spiders, unregistered species?
Ignorance? Malice? A cover-up?
In scrunching paper to set a volatile
bed, an article on refugees
and 'detainees': loss of rights,
threat of return. From twigs
to branches, the deadwood

catches: the flames rip upwards,
curling into the flue-pipe: the rip-roar
is sonorous, heavy smoke
drags the gulley, tangled
in shreds of bird and fold, combustible
residue of mountain-light.
Warming the house for the others,
you can pretend you care
about most things. Sparks
cauterise daylight. Contrary,
the pungent smell of burning,
thought of ash over garden,
the 'coming clean', denial
of cold and darkness.

Boustrophedon

Green tinge of fallow fields, tripartite,
over the shoulder the plough lines;
movement within the furrows is texture
and colour, growth might be life.

Slow release granules, implicate rate
and boldness, a serif font as misleading
as the King James version of Genesis.
Modified, it begins here. There are no endings,

regardless of culture. Placator, colloquial,
emphatic; as insignia, this inscriptor.
All writing is in the tattoo, crust
breaking through as under and emergent

the bright picture, glowing even on a dull
day; as with the page, the fences verify
occupation: written here, but wandering.
Curved and finished, ink of serotonin . . .

remember, the tractor here, aching neck
and shoulders, agistment of machine and speech.
To look for this as much as scrub or forest?
It opens out, and runs, as the indelible pencil

did in childhood, never staying as it should.
The words of the sprayboom are diffuse,
and the edges of contours and furrows invert—
there is nothing said or implied beyond

saturation here. These field-lines cannot grow,
cannot support search patterns and prayers;
dark rites are just fear, and so complete
the sheen, more imagined. Small plots feed

the corporate, sharp cold southerlies
remembered as a growing season steps up a gear,
body clock sounding off, speaking loud
and quiet and over-confidently in the paddocks.

The Burning of the Hay Stacks

'Laved in the flame as in a Sacrament . . .'
                              —Thomas Merton

There was a rash of burnings
that autumn—the arson squad
said circumstances were suspicious,
but there was a lack of evidence
to pursue a prosecution.

Always at evening, in heavy weather,
humidity insisting something happen.
Storms came later, but there was no lightning
to blame. And the pattern pushed
the odds out of orbit: with a bit

of imagination, you could make five
points with the town as the centre.
Pentacle, Pentecost, pent-up energy.
The wick lit, they just erupted,
traces of sap crackling like trees

rundown by bushfire. At a point
above the stacks a blue halo, wavering
circle that looped down over the last light
of days just not right for seeding.
On the fifth occasion, the owners

of one property called on the Anglican
minister to do a blessing, and then, for good
measure, the Catholic priest. An old aunt
suggested looking back into the Old
Testament, talking persistently

about Jerusalem belonging to all religions,
of plagues and desert and exile,
her long-dead husband's Jewish roots
lost to the fires, the hidden fuel
that feeds the burning of hay stacks.

Salt Lesson

for Katherine
Ironically, the salt is the last sanctuary for animals and birds in
   the wheatbelt . . .

This patch I caretake with words
is 'kind of beautiful', as you say,
the last bit likely to go, vulnerable
within its stockade of trees.

On each side, wheat and sheep, cross-roads
locking it into place, the salinity
broken up by cuts, soil feasible
when exposed to air—light empties

the crystals at this time of year.
Winter—and the run-off from fertile
paddocks makes deltas in the salt's centre—
pools and gulleys that will seal summer.

Taking an inventory of lifeforms, hordes
hidden where tractor and sheepdogs rarely stray,
rare birds prosper amongst the soluble
leftovers of fences and houses—

the family went there first . . . swords
and ploughshares are rank jokes as the feral
cat moves in bursts, the fox digs in, accountable
to field mice tunnelling islands of grass

constantly. Cycling over and over,
brine-smell and acrid skin coating, fur
matted . . . registering an intruder.

Chainsaw

The seared flesh of wood, cut
to a polish, deceives: the rip and tear
of the chain, its rapid cycling
a covering up of raw savagery.
It is not just machine. In the blur
of its action, in its guttural roar,
it hides the malice of organics.
Cybernetic, empirical, absolutist.
The separation of Church and State,
conspiracies against the environmental
lobby, enforcement of fear, are at the core
of its modus operandi. The cut of softwood
is deceptive, hardwood dramatic: just
before dark on a chill evening
the sparks rain out—dirty wood,
hollowed by termites, their digested
sand deposits, capillaried highways
imploded: the chainsaw effect.
It is not subtle. It is not ambient.
It is trans nothing. A clogged airfilter
has it sucking up more juice—
it gargles, floods, chokes
into silence. Sawdust dresses boots,
jeans, the field. Gradually
the paddock is cleared, the wood
stacked in cords along the lounge-room wall.
A darkness kicks back and the cutout
bar jerks into place, a distant chainsaw
dissipates. Further on, some seconds later,
another does the same. They follow

the onset of darkness, a relay of severing,
a ragged harmonics stretching back
to its beginning—gung-ho,
blazon, overconfident. Hubristic
to the final cut, last drop of fuel.

Against Depression

As polluted as this place might be,
Let's plant trees and encourage birds,
Encircle the salt and crop in thirds,
Let dead river gums enhance the heronry.

Small bush reserves might expand;
Mount Bakewell be left to stand
For itself, its rare alpine plants
Safe from microwaves and 'best use' rants,

To be known by its indigenous name—
Walwalinj—on government maps;
To fill those elusive gaps
In the GM-plan with an organic scheme.

The Early Onset of Darkness

Winter has little if nothing
To do with it; the first to go
Is the cloched light of the 'gulley',
Gazetted for a road, mock-hollow
Between paddock and fencing.

It is imagined foxes know
This counterpoint to light,
Awaken with day's closing, but internally
Realise the red-orange fringe, bright
On the range's granite edge, slow

In memory, as slow as it is rapid
In recollection. And then the mid-ground
With its tapering gradient, valley
Walls balancing quadratic sound
Within the visual equation, a grid

Of darkness overlaying the canopies
Of York gum stands and patches of parrot
Bush; the final stage is not a scree
Of crows calibrating a summit,
But bristling metal of antennas

Networking the district. Redress
Of equivocal connection, the radiant air
Inside the cells of the disconnected body,
An irritant, an afterthought, the glare
Of headlights coming out of blankness.

Land Leased Back to Themselves

for John

1. Budgies

The bark drying out of the fog
crackles—trees vibrate
with heat exchange. A pair
of budgies feeds between furrows
on land leased back to themselves,
a reinvestment in longevity,
perching on fence-posts
and augmenting, balancing
on rusted strands of barbed wire
over the salt run-off. Flock-birds,
they scan and sharply angle
the low sky with flights
of piercing intensity.
For us, at least, it's unusual—
a witnessing.

2. Polluted Well

Dynamic Lifter, label up, prismic film
on brackish water—recorded
as text this well since I was a child.
Back most years, briefly.
Lichen-topped rim, fallen fence,
grey wood in splinters, the dry
stone wall of the well a pressured
circle—conglomerate, quartz, chunks
of granite—dead grass—rat holes,

       undercurrents.

Netting from fruit trees

holds the lens, the optic nerve,
animus gazing up through the murky stuff
of settlement, parrots dropping clusters
from flowering gums ripped up anyway
by bee swarms in psychedelic
exultation. Wire bandwidth
strands in gauges, hot connection
to rusted roots eaten through varieties
of figuratives, as if to endorse
TALON!—rodenticide—'bury
all rodent bodies and ensure . . .
DO NOT use in wet situations . . .
DO NOT allow baits to come in contact with water . . .
DO NOT apply baits to crops . . .';
no longer water but liquid metal,
old prams and tines in necklaces,
teeth dulled beneath the splintered
crossbeam, the place of drawing,
gaping mouth and uneven dentures
oxymorons.

3. Dam
Shallowing, the filling in, tin
from old shed suppressed
in limpid water—railway
sleepers, coils of wire.
Sheep bones—a carcass
rots 'cleaner' in salty water . . .
signs the fox has tried to drink
and hunt here. Banks levelling,
budgies in the flowering gums,
this transitional world of pairs
and single trees.

4. Collapsed shed, wattle birds
on the catatonic
hay baler . . . the artistic
would call it sculpture,
even though its rust
might carry tetanus. Rose quartz
loosens bonds, chips
and shatters. Jarrah crossbeams
weathered, but split (for some reason)
recently, sport in bloodshed.
Grass-thin year. Up through twisted
eyebolts, earthy stumps.
What responds to childhood?
Corrugated iron that in summer
harbours dugites? Tree as wide as family
dug-out to feed the horses, closed off
at each end by sheets of tin,
as thin as paper.

Miracle at New Norcia

In a hard place Our Lady's counsel is the straining
of syrinxes fused, furls of ignition and combustion,
all birds' exclamations hurled into passion, raining

particles composited from eyes and conflagration,
relics and sacristy, strychnine and vestments,
seeds just beyond the range of heat, each a station

or heart translated, her breath strong out of the vents,
out of Dom Salvado's impressive mouth, shrine-
maker, prayers that change wind's direction without
   ambivalence;

flames back on flames, a hot embolism, sign
of sent flames, exasperated, depleted, emptied;
gaze upon this phantasm, doctrinaire line

months in getting back, against this house freed
from Satan's urging towards it, as we retell
it, as part of wheatbelt miscellany, our greed

for crossover myths and stories, hard sell
prayers that play their politics, right-wing
politicians on display in the roadhouse, the hotel

with its cells under new management. Sing
psalms to olives and scrub, the blistering heat—
the searing kind that gets under skin, cauterising

and lifting like paint, art patron; that will entreat
the last hay cut and folded and tied out of sibilant
rows, the spark that an hour earlier would have brought

a miracle to its knees? Small community, prominent
as resin and chiaroscuro, swept over, light dampened
in blackening polkas of conversion, the cant

of faith, music of Rome and Spain, island
of twisted filaments on the river's edge where
language comes into its own and children see sand

become mud as the firestorm lifts and the air
leaves them gasping for breath, their stories
mixed into the bread which rises contraire.

Imitations of Sign and Subjectivity in York: or why I despair of poetry having any meaning beyond the page

Snakeskin shucked and pinned under tin shed walls
almost flat on the ground, a seasonal
thing to do with body-size and age; near
here I stood watering bush beans and snow

peas when a light plane flying towards Mount
Bakewell faltered—its single engine stalled,
starved of fuel, foil to good engineering,
deadpan counter-measure, technology

lethally flawed—most of the folks in York
are in favour of war, or the idea
of war, and will vote accordingly . . . cut
dead. I watched 'in horror', then ran, then glanced

back to see it drift and hear the pilot
struggling with the ignition; past moments
failed linearity, and 'time' earmarked
intense self-deception, alternately

saying events exist before/after
within the quantitative universe,
but realising the trite and shallow
New Age tone of such considerations—

spark!—I heard it restart, and watched it lift.
Geometric panels of shed snakeskin
retain an olive-brown tone, though this place
has not long seen olives fall, the soil is brine

in the wet—recently they have become
a popular if slow-to-yield cash crop.
In keeping with the 'Mediterranean'
decor of the region, a dugite snake's

shedding almost six feet of deadish skin
by imperial measure, which number
revolutions like tree-rings, which metrics
will never delete from history. It's

to do with vulgarity, mood changes,
arrogance, and despotism either
side of the firebreaks—truth is, it's not
potential fires but the effort to cut

them short, to create a thin brown and beige
line around fodder, crops, trees, and homestead.
The rainwater tank will be delivered
next Friday and the shed roof has to be

washed thoroughly to remove as much spray-
drift as possible—thanks to neighbouring
farmlets, the saturated atmosphere
rendering 'organic certified' just

absurd, though we must try. So, can I say
I'm a vegan anarchist pacifist
without being rhetorical, without
the verse turning into a polemic?

The rip of the prop cuts crow and parrot,
spliced in the deadly aqua of these skies.
Our nerves just can't hack it. This interface
of tense in language and activity

is lampooned in hay paddocks—concentric
windfalls, illiterate circles that'd
pattern firetalk, deadly as Swinburne
to non-air-travelling Victorian

sensibilities, hermaphroditic
nature of hay-making—all ingestion,
ejaculation, compression, binding
and fractals of moisture levels. A wide

choice of bales and even hand-bound sheaves
stooked as souvenirs for weekend gazings
of poets cruising the countryside. Can
I really loathe them? I doubt it, I doubt

it because of the kind of heat beneath
garden mulch—out of keeping with the heat
of exposed surfaces. Humidity,
breeding ground for bacteria, is passed

over or ends in the rapid cycling
of a willy-willy working the dust
like iron filings: electro-magnetic
mini-twisters, swirls of figuration.

Really, all I need say is that each night
as the train passes over the crossing
a short way from here, I map elegies
I can never write. The teenager torn

by grain wagons—the weight on a single
wheel is phenomenal and tempered steel
cuts through consciousness—to be dragged for miles
before the driver realised, wrecks lyric.

Poetry is a craft that can be learned,
but failings of grammar and syntax can
open whole new fields of 'truth' and 'insight';
words enjambed and paratactical play

hitch the field-machine to the tractor, lines
hydraulics controlling depth and angles,
pressure a cell of disruptive air, wind-
sheer, callous art. Much of this hay is for

export, to work the balance of payments.
The same plane that momentarily failed
has been back in the sky since—serviced or
at least checked over one would guess. The last

few days have been unsettled, though it will
become steadily hotter. Lightning strikes
are a risk, especially given high
grass around the house, shut in by firebreaks,

the snake with new skin—somewhere pursuing
small mice that multiply during summer,
come out of the house to feast on the grass seeds,
abundant and labile in this climate.

The View

Depressed in late green, the lakes
concentrate, buffer sand walls
and steel gates, to entertain
and congregate the Beverley Ski Club.
Waders walk on water, and nature reserve
means shotgun shells decay detonators out,
corrosive imprimaturs exposed, flights
of ducks keeping low, riveted
against the sun. Mulga parrots graze
among litanies of micro snail shells,
fossils, scarce seed among litter,
country that will only photograph
through a red filter. Language
chokes here, so far from the coast,
and signs make visceral static
of rest and recreation. LandCare: a belt
of eucalypts infringing pasture,
tentative plantings cowering
by cattle grids. Anger—emotional
vacuum—undoes metaphor,
though the trees are barely allegorical,
tense against forests of sharp grey needles
lampooning complex light, density
of saline water. What's rare
highlights our failures, glimpses
of repair in a life of green carpets:
emptiness full in memory, adrenaline
delineating saltbush and laughter,
indifference of speedboat interior
reverberating through the wheatbelt,
blurring the view and desiderata.

Location Triggers

The pillared porch, Corinthian
because it's easiest from books,
plastered, upholding world's ceiling
that goes through to the next story
always colder in winter, maybe cooler in summer,
airflow and loveseat, swinging
where foliage redresses trees
in gendered avenues, sweeping uphill
as around flat fields, the grey rot
of corn stalks, Japanese beetle
driving towards modification, it's said,
avoiding upper rooms where heat unsettles
small windows, vicarious
and remembering a purple rising light,
hillfolds and outcrops bettered
by kites and glider, their freedom
paramount over scrub and small animals
they'd destroy, farmers alarmed
by drop-ins, all land there
like thermals and updrafts, but suddenly
undercut, we resist calling it revenge,
colluding with indifferent Nature,
visa and permit, green card
as crops spread: they won't let me
into their pastoral entirely,
invited to ride the header,
to harvest cobs and interiors
that exchange chemical appearance;
protectionist policies and markets
fill supermarket aisles, fill
hunting and trapping magazines,

fur around collars, covering
cold ears, addressing steers
on Texan clichés, clinging like ideas
of Kansas. We take back leaf-litter
stirring in warmer years, lack of snowdrifts,
birds chopping and changing
or not there at all: correlations so easy,
suppressed to keep mystery
intact . . . or fenceless plurals
full of Wallace Stevens,
growing randomly and imitating
gardens, as if you'd fly straight
from Columbus to Paris, or get diverted
to New Orleans, or Baton Rouge;
I track these infinitudes,
connect nouns from an uncle's paddocks
in places threatened by closure,
by tariffs, sucked into global
silos and temptations,
cantons and guilds and red barns
lit by nuclear light,
as fission is comradeship,
alliance, the blind leading the blind,
and grain swelling on lightless nights,
Biblical texts written with a human hair
on rice, as faith makes cars run
and the fringes shutdown:
deny all access.

Across the Gravel Wastes, A Farmer Views His Neighbour Stealing His Last Water on the Sabbath Day

The Top Dam is down to white lines—
Summer over, these are the signs;
Quail as cipher amongst stubble,
Fixed on water over gravel.

The red ute's windscreen charred by heat,
Light-seared Psalter left on the seat,
A parched neighbour fears the trouble,
Fixed on water over gravel.

Sweating to fill tanks unnoticed,
His theft in conscience soon excused,
He drains brine to a blurred puddle,
Fixed on water over gravel.

Seen from the house as the storm breaks,
Flood of rain turning fields to lakes,
The crime is lodged deep in the will,
Fixed on water over gravel.

Mulga Parrots

for Rod Smith

Subtle birds, canvassing
salt wastes for seeds,
brilliant array of colours
squeezed through reeds
of clarinets, the bleak lake
rippling with simultaneity.

Their relationship
to Yenyenning is discreet,
and sympathy is outside
our hearing, thin scrubland
a habitat where vigilance
brings rewards for foraging,

where undulating flight
takes them to high branches
of trees resisting poison,
each pair as one: russet,
yellow, orange, emerald green
and olive-brown; the sounds

of imploded suns,
evening-light at midday.

Flight

A wagtail darts into the shed at all angles
from trusses and supports, hovering in corners,
twitching with what seems to be semi-confidence
on boxes of books, its insect search more intense
than fear of my presence; but fear is reaction
and reading it tells you nothing of the causes
beyond the obvious, the precedents that build
histories of caution and sensitivity:
this flight within the building, dizzying flight plan,
short passages strung together, accumulation
of the random and the planned. The wagtail has done
this before, knowing the location of objects,
that shed corners are likely insect hotspots—gnats,
mosquitoes, flies, and a paper wasp weathering
the first days of winter, sluggish and extremely
vulnerable, and spiders playing the advocate's
role, also waiting both ways, this internal flight.
Outside, single-engine Cessnas and Pilatus
Porters—ex-military—lumber through gauze cloud,
encircling the mountain, then unloading over
the drop zone, jumpers descending seeds infesting
paddocks surrounding their targets, the wind stirring
then denying its presence. Every few minutes
the drone comes 'round, as last crops are set to boggy
ground, those who waited just too long, the quality
and yield of grain a game of chance, intuition,
experience. The wagtail jinks out into light.
Flu weather, air pockets shifting, overlaying . . .
the bird's thin legs have you thinking fragility
like tenterhooks, or tenuous point-taking, or
pivoting on a detail of theology,

the operator of machinery no more
socially minded than enigmatic, that's flight
or a variety of palaver within
the germinal, unfurling across the furrows,
the boggy soil, integrated into the ups
and downs of walking, even gentle traversing.
The telegraph is down to zero, sidetracking
railway line and freight trains in the hours before
dawn. And some birds even then, night birds' cryptic song . . .
countering the morning birds of the Cambridge fens.
For safety on lonely roads his partner carries
a mobile telephone—reception tentative.
Weight for weight, the body has that dizzy feeling,
intense giddiness of seemingly proper speech,
as if words should be ordered; skittish eye and ear,
such tiny claws, species without social conscience?
Polyrhythmic, auxiliary, scattered clauses
pied and dissolute nations of dexterity:
target, flight-path, fly-catch, out before we know it!

The Killing Tree

The great limb of the flooded gum
        tourniqueted by chain, a sluice
in gravel feeding into a drain,
        and down to the river.

They haven't killed for years,
        though the sap of all trees runs
bloody here—'It's a piece of our
        time, constraining

the rings of history. This is
        our garden where we fell,
where we rose again—a vestigial
        memory.' The sheep bled,

and the bleeding spread, filling
        the sun on an evening
horizon. Alive with ants and flies
        the blade mocked the moon,

its frosts. A pet lamb that outgrew
        the children and broke away
from the Coke bottle and rubber teat
        bled abundantly.

All atoms larger than they look.
        Red shift, emptied,
getting slower about the rippled
        wound, the chain

growing older, anatomically wise.
      Wedding. Te deum.
Swinging on a whim the chain
raddles the hands—here,
      where they killed.

Removing the Fox Baits

It is doubly
ironic that a fastidious
couple, rigid and hot
at the thought
of poison,
haunted and tormented
by the idea of meat,
should track
the ranger
doing his rounds,
scrutinise his mannerisms,
his process of laying
baits, move in
a few steps behind him
and lift the baits
in gloved and pincered hands,
to seal in a bag
for incineration.
The sound of diminution,
the quoll and native mouse,
are heard in the space
of each breath—
the ranger exuding
a hunter's sweat,
as body warmth
levers conscience,
and a fox death
contorts the tense.

Cold

The coldest spot at Wheatlands was down
Where family ashes were interred, where a massive
York gum riddled with lead from target practice

Held back the salt: the bottleneck, last line
Of defence in settler immolation.
With the sun frosting crops, glare

Coming out of florescence, cold flowed up
From the dead and drew on the warmth
Of blood channelled through narrow veins, an exchange

That brought a shiver or shudder
That said death is just on hold. Parrots
And small birds you don't name, *Op. cit.*

Chill with friction in their songs—sound
Before thought, light signalling
Switches in rhythms, registers

Of trauma—this fringe of low ground,
Ashes in marginal soil, too sub to reconstitute,
Held in stasis in their polymeric boxes.

Aftershocks

There have been at least fifty aftershocks
since yesterday's quake, which coincided
with a particularly vicious cold front,
perverse revenge for a dry winter.

Lines packed close together, non-gliding
birds catch the wind or it catches them,
and tossed over fragments of bush
disorientate; thin trees bearing up as thickset

classifications crack and fissure from inner
rings out; a rufous songlark flies low near
the house, intent on insects clinging to barely
sheltered spots, standing water rippling

in gravel shallows, seismographs or omens,
volatile membranes holding the district together.

Liminal Devotional

Per omnia secula saeculorum . . .

Whereupon in service
go you or I, refrained against the light,
the show-through of texts upon the page,
geographies of stanza shape: these hymns
we broadcast in times less bright,
work as ozone, as
ultra-violet.

Index of Titles and First Lines

A bounty of 'fame throughout the district and no, 66

A Council-approved replacement, 19

Across the dark fields the family is spread, 63

Across the Gravel Wastes, A Farmer Views His Neighbour Stealing His Last Water on the Sabbath Day, 180

Aerial View of Wheatlands in Mid-Autumn, An, 69

Aftershocks, 188

After Sir Lawrence Alma-Tadema's 94° in the Shade (1876), 79

Against Depression, 166

a lack of water drives you to the well, 87

Anathalamion, 54

An easterly stretches and compresses, 12

A pair of painted quails, 13

Approaching the Anniversary of my Last Meeting with my Son, 58

A ring-necked parrot drops into flight, 11

Ascension of Sheep, The, 32

As if it just slipped from under me, 150

Asked about the wandoo, 50

As polluted as this place might be, 166

A wagtail darts into the shed at all angles, 182

Back from England and fenland, 76

Bark-stripped upper branches, 101

Bermuda Triangle, The, 75

Black Suns, 8

Blue clouds scuttle the eucalypt sun, 45

Bluff Knoll Sublimity, 48

Bottlebrush Flowers, The, 19

Boustrophedon, 159

Branches, The, 100

Burning of the Hay Stacks, The, 161

Cardinal Influences Peripheral Sight, A, 111

Chainsaw, 164

Chambers: Prison Cells beneath the Nineteenth-Century Country Mansion, Western Australia, The, 116

Chilli Catharsis, 26

Cleared land is a place of weeds, 83

Cold, 187

Comes before the house—domicile, 143

Crane and Hawk, 7

Crest, The, 154

Cultures, 115

Deployed against the snow, 109

Depressed in late green, the lakes, 177

Diagnostics, 114

Distance brings thoughts of the driveway at York, 132

Down below the dam, 5

drought, 87

Drowning in Wheat, 64

Dust particles cling to sweat despite the sun just up, 71

Early Onset of Darkness, The, 167

Eclogue on a Well, 21

Field Notes from Mount Bakewell, 101

Fifth Essay on Linguistic Disobedience, 136

Finches, 5

First Essay on Linguistic Disobedience, 126

Flight, 182

Fog, 42

For all its lymphatic nature, 42

Fourth Essay on Linguistic Disobedience, 134

Funeral Oration, 88

Gift, The, 125

Goading Storms Out of a Darkening Field, 44

Graffiti the indicative mood, 89

Grave, 60

Green tinge of fallow fields, tripartite, 159

Hay Bale Collected Off Road, 155

Hectic Red, 85

He's polite looking over the Polaroids, 30

Hockney's Doll Boy at the Local Country Women's Association Annual Musical: Wheatbelt, Western Australia, 80

Hölderlin was not Mad, 89

House Eclogue, 120

Hunt, The, 66

Il faut cultiver notre jardin, 83

Imitations of Sign and Subjectivity in York: or why I despair of poetry having any meaning beyond the page, 173

Imposing sharecropper or woodcuts, 148

In a darkness without chemiluminescence, 116

In a hard place Our Lady's counsel is the straining, 171

I never write 'confessional' poetry, 58

Inland, 9

Inland: storm tides, 9

In the reciprocity of summer, 69

It fortifies my blood, 26

It is doubly, 186

It's stark white in this hard, 57

It's the roads we blame for progress, 155

Killing Tree, The, 184

Land Leased Back to Themselves, 168

Lighting the Bushman Fire Before the Others Rise, 157

Lightning Tree, 57

Liminal Devotional, 189

Links, 3

Locating the ensign normative on the questboat, 151

Location Triggers, 178

Lorca and Baudrillard, protagonists, real possessors, looking for refreshment, 129

Lyrical Unification in Gambier, 112

Machine of the Twentieth Century Rolls Through the High-Yielding Crop, The, 71

Melt is variable, tacks grass tufts and declines, 138

Memorandum: 'The soul is a region without definite boundaries,' 136

Miracle at New Norcia, 171

Mulga Parrots, 181

My parents dead & the family property, 54

Myth of the Grave, The, 13

Off-centre, the weaver finch, 114

Of Writing at Wheatlands, 50

Old Hands/New Tricks, 11

On Entering Your Thirty-First Year, 27

On the Rejection of the Term
    "Property" for This Place, 151
Opening night. As the curtain lifts,
    80
Orange trees cling, 18
Orchardist, The, 18
Outflanked by the sheep run, wild
    oats, 22
Oyster catchers, 23

Parrot Deaths: Rites of Passage, 45
Pat Rafter, saviour of Australian
    tennis, 75
Pillars of Salt, 15
Pipeline, 17
Plumburst, 20
Poem for Those at Wheatlands, 38
Poetry is not the only thing, 62
Poltergeist House Eclogue, 123
Predominance of Red, The, 109
Punctured sole-skin, game of
    Twister, 141

Quartz sparks randomly, 85

Removing the Fox Baits, 186
Road to Brookton—on the nature of
    memory, The, 76
Rock Picking: Building Cairns, 36

Salt Lesson, 163
Sanctus, Sanctum: a love poem, 96
Sculpting a Poem from the Landscape's
    Painting, 33
Second Essay on Linguistic
    Disobedience: the masculine
    houses of America and waver-
    ing Australian echoes . . . , 129
Semiotics of a Truck Overturned on
    Fog, The, 150
Serpentine. Tracy asks me to stop,
    60
Seventh Essay on Linguistic Dis-
    obedience: Rejection of Land-
    scape through Body-Map, 141

Shed, The, 143
She stirs the waters, 21
Shoes once shod in a blacksmith's shop,
    82
Silo, The, 39
Sine qua non, 99
Sixth Essay on Linguistic
    Disobedience: 100 days after
    the inauguration of the men
    who advise Bush, 138
Skeleton weed/generative grammar,
    46
Skippy Rock, Augusta: Warning, the
    undertow, 23
Skylab and The Theory of Forms, 73
Snakeskin shucked and pinned
    under tin shed walls, 173
Snow so fine trees titanium white,
    125
Solitary Activities, 62
Subtle birds, canvassing, 181
Sun crisp on the curve of Bakewell,
    157

Taking the fifth, he avoided the
    traffic. The organism, 134
Tenebrae, 61
That at high speed this rise, 154
The bark drying out of the fog,
    168
The coldest spot at Wheatlands
    was down, 187
The country in summer. The tem-
    perature hovers, 79
The crane, eyes fixed, moves
    steadily, 7
The dash to the peak anaesthetizes,
    48
The grave is a gate you send flow-
    ers through, 88
The great limb of the flooded gum,
    184
The house yard harbours plumes of
    rust-faced dock concentrated,
    33

The islands are low to the water, 115

The 'I' takes in what is said—, 46

The less I see the bird, 126

The neat greens of Monument Hill, 20

The orchard, canker-bound and fading—Australian, 8

The pillared porch, Corinthian, 178

The pipeline cleaves the catchment, 17

There are days when the world, 3

There have been at least fifty aftershocks, 188

There was a rash of burnings, 161

The saturation of your art, 27

The seared flesh of wood, cut, 164

The smallest measure of matter, 96

The spine is best kept straight—, 36

The sun has dragged, 32

The Top Dam is down to white lines—, 180

The widow presupposes faux brick, 146

They'd been warned, 64

They stripped the last trees, 41

Third Essay on Linguistic Disobedience, 132

This patch I caretake with words, 163

This wooden frame might be your own, 120

Those apples I've struggled to write, 99

Through insect screens, 111

Through Vertical Blinds, 146

Trial, The, 148

Two Days Before Harvest, 12

View, The, 177

Visitors, as if they knew, never remarked, 39

Walking at night, blank stone, 100

Warhol at Wheatlands, 30

We always look back, 15

We didn't make it but we ended up getting it, 73

What remains barely the weather, 112

Wheatbelt Gothic or Discovering a Wyeth, 22

Whereupon in service, 189

Why They Stripped the Last Trees from the Banks of the Creek, 41

Wild Radishes, 63

Winter has little if nothing, 167

You are on the verge, 61

You only realise, 38

You wait until we're alone in the house, 123